Following Christ...
The Man of God

A Study of John 6-14

FROM THE BIBLE-TEACHING MINISTRY OF

Charles R. Swindoll

INSIGHT FOR LIVING

Charles R. Swindoll graduated in 1963 from Dallas Theological Seminary, where he now serves as the school's fourth president, helping to prepare a new generation of men and women for the ministry. Chuck has served in pastorates in three states: Massachusetts, Texas, and California, including almost twenty-three years at the First Evangelical Free Church in Fullerton, California. He is currently senior pastor of Stonebriar Community Church in Frisco, Texas, north of Dallas. His sermon messages have been aired over radio since 1979 as the *Insight for Living* broadcast. A best-selling author, he has written numerous books and booklets on many subjects.

Editor in Chief:
Cynthia Swindoll

Coauthor of Text:
Ken Gire

Author of Living Insights, Senior Editor, and Assistant Writer:
Wendy Peterson

Editors:
Christina Grimstad
Karla Lenderink

Copy Editor:
Marco Salazar

Rights and Permissions:
The Meredith Agency

Graphic System Administrator:
Bob Haskins

Director, Communications Division:
John Norton

Print Production Manager:
Don Bernstein

Project Coordinator:
Jennifer Hubbard

Printer:
Sinclair Printing Company

Unless otherwise identified, all Scripture references are from the New American Standard Bible, copyright © The Lockman Foundation 1960, 1962, 1963, 1968, 1971, 1972, 1973, 1975, 1977. Used by permission. Scripture taken from the Holy Bible, New International Version, Copyright © 1973, 1978, 1984 International Bible Society, used by permission of Zondervan Bible Publishers [NIV].

Based on the outlines, charts and transcripts of Charles R. Swindoll's sermons, the study guide was revised by Wendy Peterson, senior editor and assistant writer in the Educational Ministries Department of Insight for Living:

Copyright © 2000 by Insight for Living

Guide coauthored by Ken Gire:
Copyright © 1987 by Charles R. Swindoll, Inc.
Outlines published by New Standard for Living and Insight for Living titled *The Gospel of John:*
Copyright © 1975, 1976 by Charles R. Swindoll, Inc.
Original outlines, charts, and transcripts for series titled *The Gospel of John*:
Copyright © 1975, 1976 by Charles R. Swindoll, Inc.

An effort has been made to locate sources and obtain permission where necessary for the quotations used in this book. In the event of any unintentional omission, a modification will gladly be incorporated in future printings.

ISBN 1-57972-329-2
Cover design by Michael Standlee Design
Cover image © Daryl Benson/Masterfile Corp.
Printed in the United States of America

Contents

Introduction

The center section of John's Gospel allows us to walk with Christ through numerous scenes. He faces criticism, defends a helpless woman, gives sight to the blind, teaches His disciples, raises the dead, and models humility by washing His disciples' feet. No one who closely follows Jesus can remain the same.

Travel with me through these events. Use your imagination. Think of yourself as being a part of each scene. Don't miss one detail. You will find that Jesus' godly qualities are contagious. So be forewarned! Your life will begin to change.

As we study Christ's life, let's be careful not to limit our thoughts or to concentrate our attention only on the printed page. These are living truths designed to get inside our lives. Let's allow them entrance.

Chuck Swindoll

Chuck Swindoll

Putting Truth Into Action

Knowledge apart from application falls short of God's desire for His children. He wants us to apply what we learn so that we will change and grow. This study guide was prepared with these goals in mind. As you go through the following pages, we hope your desire to discover biblical truth will grow as your understanding of God's Word increases, and that you will be encouraged to apply what you've learned.

To assist you in your study, we've included a section called 🌿 **Living Insights** at the end of each lesson. These exercises will challenge you to study further and to think of specific ways to put your discoveries into action.

There are many ways to use this guide—in personal devotions, group studies, discussions with friends and family, and Sunday school classes. And, of course, it's an ideal study aid when you're listening to its corresponding *Insight for Living* radio series.

To benefit most from this study guide, we would encourage you to consider it a spiritual journal. That's why we've included space in the **Living Insights** for recording your thoughts and discoveries. We hope you'll return to those sections often for review and encouragement as you continue to grow in your walk with Christ.

Insight for Living

Following Christ...
The Man of God

A STUDY OF JOHN 6-14

JOHN

	Deity	God-Man	Ministry	Discourse	Trials and Death	Empty Tomb	Assurance
	"The Word was God." (1:1)	"The Word became flesh." (1:14)	Miraculous signs: Heals invalid at Bethesda (5) Feeds 5,000 (6) Walks on water (6) Heals blind man (9) Raises Lazarus (11)	Private talks: Servanthood (13) Heaven (14) Abiding (15) Promises (16) Prayer (17)	Crucifixion	Private talks: Appearances (20)	Private talks: Future (21)
		Miraculous signs: Water into wine (2) Heals official's son (4)					
	CHAPTER 1:1–13	CHAPTERS 1:14–4:54	CHAPTERS 5–12	CHAPTERS 13–17	CHAPTERS 18–19	CHAPTER 20	CHAPTER 21
							EPILOGUE
Stage	Prologue	Acceptance	Conflict	Preparation	Crucifixion	Triumph	
			CHANGE				
Audience	Public message			Private message			
Time	Three years			Several days			
Jesus' Seven "I Am" Statements	• "I am the bread of life." (6:35) • "I am the Light of the world." (8:12) • "I am the door." (10:9) • "I am the good shepherd." (10:11)			• "I am the resurrection and the life." (11:25) • "I am the way, and the truth, and the life." (14:6) • "I am the true vine." (15:1)			
Main Theme and Key Verse	"These have been written so that you may believe that Jesus is the Christ, the Son of God; and that believing you may have life in His name." (20:31)						

Chapter 1

God's Specialty: Impossibilities

John 6:1–21

Impossibilities. Everyone can list a few. You can't make a silk purse out of a sow's ear. You can't get blood out of a turnip. You can't make a crab walk straight.

Yet Jesus knit His apostolic purse out of the frayed threads of local fishermen and tax gatherers; He got wine out of ordinary tap water; and He made a man, thirty-eight years lame, to walk. Impossible? The word wasn't even in Christ's vocabulary.

How about your vocabulary? Do words like *can't . . . won't work . . . impossible* leap from your lips? Has a pessimistic outlook imprinted these words in your mind? What's on your list of impossibilities? Your marriage, your job, your finances?

In this chapter, we're going to see Jesus perform two more impressive, impossible feats—the feeding of the five thousand and walking on water. If He can do these, imagine what He can do with your life and your impossibilities!

I. A Question of Perspective

Many times the issue of impossibility depends on our perspective. For example, to a child, many things seem impossible, like baking or long division. But from an adult vantage point, these things are not only possible but can be handled with relative ease. Let's try to understand the impossible by looking at it from two different viewpoints, the human and the divine.

    A. The human perspective. Webster defines *impossible* as "incapable of being or of occurring . . . insuperably difficult."[1] Many of our circumstances seem hopeless when viewed horizontally.

    B. The divine perspective. From the vertical perspective, however, nothing is too heavy to lift when God holds the lever. The prophet Jeremiah makes that claim in his Old Testament book.

        "Ah Lord God! Behold, Thou hast made the heavens

---

1. *Merriam-Webster's Collegiate Dictionary,* 10th ed., see "impossible."

1

and the earth by Thy great power and by Thine
outstretched arm! Nothing is too difficult for Thee."
(Jer. 32:17)
God confirms Jeremiah's words later in the chapter.

"Behold, I am the Lord, the God of all flesh; is anything too difficult for Me?" (v. 27)
And with resounding clarity, the New Testament echoes this
promise.

"For nothing will be impossible with God."
(Luke 1:37)
"The things impossible with men are possible with
God." (18:27)
Two threads of truth run through both Testaments. One, God's
power is unlimited. Two, God's promise is unconditional.
Nothing stands in His way—ever!

II. A Biblical Example

In John 6:1–15, the seemingly immovable object of human impossibility meets the irresistible force of divine power.

A. The setting. Verses 1–4 paint a backdrop for our scene.

After these things Jesus went away to the other
side of the Sea of Galilee (or Tiberias). And a great
multitude was following Him, because they were
seeing the signs which He was performing on those
who were sick. And Jesus went up on the mountain,
and there He sat with His disciples. Now the Passover, the feast of the Jews, was at hand.

Thousands of people have gathered in the area, probably today's Golan Heights, to celebrate the Passover. D. A. Carson
tells us that "the Passover feast was to Palestinian Jews what
the fourth of July is to Americans. . . . It was a rallying point
for intense, nationalistic zeal."[2] After healing the sick and
preaching to the eager crowds all day, Jesus takes the disciples
aside for some needed rest (see Mark 6:31). But the people
keep coming (John 6:5a), and their needs take priority over
any planned respite.

B. The opportunity. Great opportunities are often disguised as
unsolvable problems. Jesus and His disciples try to get away,
but a needy crowd takes precedence. Let's watch as a humanly
unsolvable problem becomes a great opportunity when seen
from a divine viewpoint.

---

2. D. A. Carson, *The Gospel according to John* (Grand Rapids, Mich.: William B. Eerdmans
Publishing Co., 1991), p. 269.

1. **From a human perspective.** With their limited, human understanding, these weary disciples can see only a swelling sea of humanity threatening to wash over them. In verse 10 we are told that this great multitude numbered five thousand men. Including women and children, this figure could have easily been eight or ten thousand.
2. **From a divine perspective.** From Jesus' point of view, the crowds weren't an infringement but an opportunity . . . a chance to reveal His glory and, at the same time, stretch His disciples' faith. He begins with a test for Philip.

> "Where are we to buy bread, that these may eat?" (v. 5b)

Jesus' intent is not to humiliate or demean Philip; rather, He wants to build Philip's muscle of faith, to help him grow and make him stronger.

A Strategy for Building Faith

Philip's test is explained by the words "for He Himself knew what He was intending to do" (v. 6b), clearly indicating that Jesus is not only in control of the immediate circumstances but several steps ahead of the game.

Like a brilliant chess player who thinks several moves ahead, Jesus plots a strategy to build the faith of His disciples. A chess player may give up a minor piece as a gambit in order to later gain an advantage, and so this King is willing to give up a little R and R for His troops in order to gain a more committed band of men.

When you realize that your circumstances, no matter how overwhelming or pressing, are ruled by a King who seeks your highest good, you can truly "consider it all joy . . . when you encounter various trials, knowing that the testing of your faith produces endurance . . . that you may be perfect and complete, lacking in nothing" (James 1:2–4).

Is that how you view circumstances that crowd you or bring unexpected pressure? Seeing things from this perspective will make it easier to see His hand at work . . . and His strategy for building your faith.

C. The test. Actually, two disciples take the test this day. Philip is appointed—Andrew volunteers.

1. Philip. With computer speed, Philip analyzes the situation and gives Jesus a spreadsheet answer.

> "Two hundred denarii worth of bread is not sufficient for them, for everyone to receive a little." (John 6:7)

A denarius was approximately a day's wages for the common laborer (Matt. 20:2). Philip is quick to come to the bottom line in terms of dollars and cents—dollars and cents they don't have, he implies. However, Philip's balance sheet doesn't show the infinite wealth and power of God, who owns the earth and all it contains (Ps. 24:1) and who can do "exceeding abundantly beyond all that we ask or think" (Eph. 3:20). So how does Philip do on his exam? Not so well. He fails in three areas. One, he sees only the situation, not the possible solution. Two, he's more concerned about the odds against them than about those for them. Three, he calculates for only a bare minimum—"for everyone to receive a little."

2. Andrew. While Philip busily burns out the batteries in his pocket calculator, Andrew scurries among the crowd looking for groceries.

> One of His disciples, Andrew, Simon Peter's brother, said to Him, "There is a lad here who has five barley loaves and two fish, but what are these for so many people?" (John 6:8–9)

Andrew, who has volunteered for this test, scores somewhat better than Philip. A careful optimist, Andrew at least seeks a solution, even though it is a human one. Putting his nose in a kid's picnic basket, he finds five flat barley loaves and a couple of pickled sardines.[3] Admittedly, it isn't much, but Andrew's approach is better than Philip's. However, he also becomes overwhelmed by the circumstances: "but what are these for so many people?"

┌─ ***Looking for Loaves in All the Wrong Places!*** ─────┐

Philip sees the impossible circumstances surrounding them and looks first at the budget. Andrew

---

3. "Barley bread was bread of a cheap kind, so the boy was probably poor. The two fishes were something of a tidbit that would make the coarse barley bread more palatable." Leon Morris, *The Gospel according to John,* rev. ed., The New International Commentary on the New Testament Series (Grand Rapids, Mich.: William B. Eerdmans Publishing Co., 1995), p. 304.

sees the same circumstances and checks the pantry.

But neither of them thinks to look to the Lord. Seems strange, doesn't it? Particularly after they have seen Him change water into wine.

But then, don't we respond in much the same way? We've all seen Jesus work miracles in our lives. We've seen Him change the old water of our lives into new wine. We've seen Him give new legs of faith to our lame spiritual bodies. Yet when faced with impossible circumstances, how soon we forget the power of our God. The next time you're faced with the impossible, try not to look at your bank account or at your Old Mother Hubbard cupboards. Look first to Jesus, the bread of life, who can do "exceeding abundantly beyond all that we ask or think."

D. The response.

1. **Jesus'.** Verses 10–13 record Jesus' miraculous response to the impossible.

> Jesus said, "Have the people sit down." Now there was much grass in the place. So the men sat down, in number about five thousand. Jesus therefore took the loaves; and having given thanks, He distributed to those who were seated; likewise also of the fish as much as they wanted. And when they were filled, He said to His disciples, "Gather up the leftover fragments that nothing may be lost." And so they gathered them up, and filled twelve baskets with fragments from the five barley loaves, which were left over by those who had eaten.

Calmly and methodically, Jesus sits the people down, dividing them into manageable groups of hundreds and fifties (see Mark 6:40). And taking the scant supply of groceries, He looks to God in prayer and multiplies the food for the masses. Not only does the lad's lunch box give everyone "a little" (John 6:7), it is enough in the hands of the Lord to give everyone "as much as they wanted" (v. 11). And not only that, there are twelve baskets full of leftovers—one for each of the disciples! Philip and Andrew are probably scratching their heads in amazement, while a poor kid with a Cheshire grin is putting his thumbs in his suspenders and rocking back on his heels.

5

2. The people's. The satisfied Passover crowd, unfortunately, wants to use Jesus toward their ends rather than learn and follow His plan.

> When therefore the people saw the sign which He had performed, they said, "This is of a truth the Prophet who is to come into the world." (v. 14)

Commentator Lesslie Newbigin illuminates the scene for us.

> The crowd had followed Jesus because they saw him as a healer, as one who could satisfy their needs. The feeding confirms their opinion. Moses, who had led Israel out of slavery and had called down manna from heaven, had also promised that the Lord would send another prophet like himself who would speak God's word (Deut. 18:15ff), and it seems to have been a common belief that he also would bring down manna from heaven. Jesus must be this promised prophet. The long-awaited day of a new deliverance is at hand. The enthusiasm of the crowd rises; they will seize him forthwith and make him their leader.[4]

Jesus, however, wants no part of their plan.

> Jesus therefore perceiving that they were intending to come and take Him by force, to make Him king, withdrew again to the mountain by Himself alone. (v. 15)

Jesus is the promised Prophet; He is the King of the Jews. So why doesn't He accept the people's support? Newbigin explains what Jesus sees—and what we often fail to see— that Jesus will reign on His terms, not on the people's or on Satan's (see Matt. 4:8–10).

> This is not faith [on the part of the crowd] but unbelief. They have not understood who Jesus is. Jesus will not be the instrument of any human enthusiasm or the symbol for any human program. To say "Jesus is king" is true if the word "king" is wholly defined by the person of Jesus; it is false and blasphemous if Jesus is made instrumental to a definition of kingship derived from elsewhere. Jesus has

4. Lesslie Newbigin, *The Light Has Come: An Exposition of the Fourth Gospel* (Grand Rapids, Mich.: William B. Eerdmans Publishing Co., 1982), pp. 75–76.

come "to proclaim liberty to the captives," but he will not become the mascot for a people's movement of liberation. At the very moment when the cry "Make Jesus king" is rending the air Jesus abruptly disappears, leaving both the crowds and the disciples with no visible goal for their enthusiasm. And on that scene of disappointed hope night falls. Jesus is alone with his Father. The crowds are left on the hillside, and the disciples are left without an answer to the question "Where has he gone?" They are—in every sense—in the dark.[5]

3. The disciples'. Probably somewhat confused by Jesus' refusal to be made king, the disciples followed His instructions anyway (Mark 6:45) and headed toward Capernaum via the Sea of Galilee.

> Now when evening came, His disciples went down to the sea, and after getting into a boat, they started to cross the sea to Capernaum. And it had already become dark, and Jesus had not yet come to them. And the sea began to be stirred up because a strong wind was blowing. When therefore they had rowed about three or four miles, they beheld Jesus walking on the sea and drawing near to the boat; and they were frightened. But He said to them, "It is I; do not be afraid." They were willing therefore to receive Him into the boat; and immediately the boat was at the land to which they were going. (John 6:16–21)

This incident, seen by the disciples only, serves two purposes. First, it shows the nature of Jesus' true kingship, where He rules over every realm, including creation. Nothing is impossible for Him—not even walking on water or calming a storm. Second, as Mark's Gospel reveals, it shows that the disciples didn't yet understand who Jesus really was. They were "greatly astonished" and "frightened" of Him (Mark 6:50–51), because "they had not gained any insight from the incident of the loaves, but their heart was hardened" (v. 52). They did not yet grasp that Jesus was God in the flesh, the sustaining Bread of Life, a truth we will see Him take great pains to explain in our next chapter.

5. Newbigin, *The Light Has Come,* p. 76.

⚘ *Living Insights*

Have you ever faced a humanly impossible situation? What was it?

_____

_____

_____

How did you handle it? Did you recognize yourself in Philip's
pessimistic look at the circumstances? Or did Andrew's discourage-
ment about meager resources ring a bell with you? Or can you
identify more with the crowds, who misread Jesus' mission and
wanted Him to do their bidding?

_____

_____

_____

_____

_____

What sort of impact did this impossibility have on your faith?
Did you feel stretched? Or broken? Did you consider that God might
be testing you, and if so, did that give you some relief or make you
angry? What happened in your attitude toward God?

_____

_____

_____

_____

_____

_____

Do you think this story of Jesus feeding the five thousand means
that He will resolve our every impossibility with a happy ending in
the here and now? Why or why not?

_____

_____

8

_____

_____

_____

_____

_____

_____

_____

Our immediate, physical needs and desires often obscure the long-term, spiritual aims God has in mind, don't they? Jesus certainly does want to nourish us, but He does not ever want to be reduced to a genie who will magically supply our every want. Remember, He gave the people bread and fish for just that one day. He refused to let the people make Him the "Bread King" so their stomachs could always be full.

Maybe that's the lesson we need to take away from these scenes in John's Gospel. That Jesus sees, cares, and can amply meet our needs, but He is sovereignly independent from human agendas. He has His own, bigger plan—but He will still calm our stormy seas, urging us all along to "not be afraid" (John 6:20) because He is here.

Chapter 2
Bread Delivered from Heaven
John 6:22-71

From 1789 to 1815, France was in the throes of a tumultuous revolution. It was a time when wealthy aristocrats traveled in extravagant carriages while ragged paupers begged on the streets. For the rich, life was a smorgasbord; for the destitute, a soup line.

Revolutionary France parallels the way many of us live our lives today. Indulgence and indigence live side by side within ourselves. We splurge on material goods, but emotionally we are poverty-stricken. We wine and dine at the finest of restaurants, but inside our spirits slowly starve.

Just as there is a physical hunger that only physical food can satisfy, so there is a deeper, spiritual hunger in the pit of the human soul that only spiritual food can nourish.

In this chapter, Jesus tells us to work not "for the food which perishes, but for the food which endures to eternal life" (John 6:27a). In doing so, He echoes the advice of Isaiah: "Why do you spend money for what is not bread, And your wages for what does not satisfy?" (Isa. 55:2a).

I. Preliminary Events
Jesus' feeding of the five thousand and His walking on water in the first part of John 6 was the lab in which He demonstrated His power over creation. In the remainder of the chapter, Jesus now takes the lab lessons and organizes them into a profound lecture that many commentators call the Bread of Life Discourse. Perhaps for the first time, the crowd that was fed the bread and fish dinner actually had all they wanted to eat (see vv. 11b-12a). It is no wonder, then, that the crowd intently followed this miracle worker. After all, where else could they find an abundance of food? Consequently, when the next day came and their hunger returned, they looked for Jesus (vv. 22-25).

II. Preeminent Issues
The miraculous feeding of the five thousand raises some important issues.

A. Clarification of motives.
First and foremost is the crowd's motive for seeking Him, which Jesus addresses in verses 26-27.

"Truly, truly, I say to you, you seek Me, not because you saw signs, but because you ate of the loaves, and were filled. Do not work for the food which perishes, but for the food which endures to eternal life, which the Son of Man shall give to you, for on

Him the Father, even God, has set His seal."[1]

Notice the contrast drawn in verse 27 between "food which perishes" and "food which endures," reminiscent of His words to the woman at the well (4:13–14). There are two kinds of hunger and two kinds of food—physical and spiritual. Jesus' point is that all these people are interested in is physical satisfaction—they're more interested in their stomachs than in their hearts, more intent on the here and now than on the hereafter.

Evaluating Your Motives

Jesus tells us in the Sermon on the Mount: "Do not be anxious for your life, as to what you shall eat, or what you shall drink; nor for your body, as to what you shall put on. Is not life more than food, and the body than clothing?" (Matt. 6:25).

Take a moment to examine your anxieties. Do you work for "food which endures," or is getting your daily bread your all-consuming passion? Jesus goes on to offer guidance for getting out of the valley of worry.

"Do not be anxious then, saying, 'What shall we eat?' or 'What shall we drink?' or 'With what shall we clothe ourselves?' For all these things the Gentiles eagerly seek; for your heavenly Father knows that you need all these things. But seek first His kingdom and His righteousness; and all these things shall be added to you." (vv. 31–33)

B. Discussion of miracles. Their mistaken motives brought to light, the crowd responds with a question that exposes their need for instruction.

"What shall we do, that we may work the works of God?" Jesus answered and said to them, "This is the work of God, that you believe in Him whom He has sent." (John 6:28–29)

---

1. Commenting on the latter part of verse 27, William Barclay notes: "It was not the *signature*, but the *seal* that authenticated. In commercial and political documents it was the seal, imprinted with the signet ring, which made the document valid; it was the seal which authenticated a will; it was the seal on the mouth of a sack or a crate that guaranteed the contents." With each miracle performed, God's authenticating seal on Christ's life was evident to all. William Barclay, *The Gospel of John,* rev. ed., The Daily Study Bible Series (Philadelphia, Pa.: Westminster Press, 1975), vol. 1, p. 213.

Jesus' answer nudges them toward an understanding of His identity—He is letting them know that He is the Messiah, the Promised One, in whom they are to place their faith and to whom they are to pledge their allegiance. But the crowd reacts with "prove-it" skepticism.

"What then do You do for a sign, that we may see, and believe You? What work do You perform?" (v. 30)

Recalling the stories they were raised on, this Jewish group digresses from "prove it" to "top this, if you're really who you say you are."

"Our fathers ate the manna in the wilderness; as it is written, 'He gave them bread out of heaven to eat.'" (v. 31)

Jesus makes it clear that Moses wasn't responsible for that wilderness bread—God was. The bread of God was a gift, whether it was shaped into manna or the Messiah (vv. 32–33). Still more attentive to their hunger pangs than to any spiritual pangs of conscience, the crowd would rather have had another loaf of bread than the abundant life within their reach.

They said therefore to Him, "Lord, evermore give us this bread." Jesus said to them, "I am the bread of life; he who comes to Me shall not hunger, and he who believes in Me shall never thirst." (vv. 34–35)

Instead of grasping the gift of salvation offered them, they hold tightly to their skepticism with closed minds and clenched hearts, as Jesus tells them:

"But I said to you, that you have seen Me, and yet do not believe. All that the Father gives Me shall come to Me, and the one who comes to Me I will certainly not cast out. For I have come down from heaven, not to do my own will, but the will of Him who sent Me. And this is the will of Him who sent Me, that of all that He has given Me I lose nothing, but raise it up on the last day. For this is the will of My Father, that everyone who beholds the Son and believes in Him, may have eternal life; and I Myself will raise him up on the last day." (vv. 36–40)

In spite of their rejection, Jesus extends the offer again.

"Truly, truly, I say to you, he who believes has eternal life. I am the bread of life. Your fathers ate the manna in the wilderness, and they died. This is the bread which comes down out of heaven, so that one may eat of it and not die. I am the living bread that came down out of heaven; if anyone eats of this bread, he shall live forever; and the bread also which I shall give for the life of the world is My flesh." (vv. 47–51)

C. Reaction of the multitude. The Jews grumble and argue (vv. 41, 52). No matter how you slice it, it just doesn't set well on their empty stomachs. So they begin to nitpick His message.

> The Jews therefore began to argue with one another, saying, "How can this man give us His flesh to eat?" (v. 52)

The mistake is as elemental as one a first-grader might make. Jesus is using a figure of speech, a metaphor. He wasn't literally bread any more than He was literally a lamb or a lion, other symbols used to describe the Messiah. He uses the symbol of bread because the inhabitants of the Ancient Near East saw it as the means for sustaining life (see Deut. 8:3). Patiently, Jesus spells it out for them.

> "Truly, truly, I say to you, unless you eat the flesh of the Son of Man and drink His blood,[2] you have no life in yourselves. He who eats My flesh and drinks My blood has eternal life, and I will raise him up on the last day. For My flesh is true food, and My blood is true drink. He who eats My flesh and drinks My blood abides in Me, and I in him. As the living Father sent Me, and I live because of the Father, so he who eats Me, he also shall live because of Me. This is the bread which came down out of heaven; not as the fathers ate, and died, he who eats this bread shall live forever." (vv. 53–58)

III. Personal Impact

At the close of this chapter, we read about three attitudes that parallel responses we see today.

A. Open defection. Many people were attracted to Jesus as a person. They were impressed by His ability to spellbind a crowd with His works and rhetoric. But when the points of His sermon got sharp, these thin-skinned followers recoiled and retreated to the back pews, and some even walked out the doors.

> Many therefore of His disciples, when they heard this said, "This is a difficult statement; who can listen

---

2. "In Jewish thought *the blood stands for the life.* It is easy to understand why. As the blood flows from a wound, life ebbs away; and to the Jew, *the blood belonged to God.* . . . When Jesus said we must drink his blood he meant that we must take his life into the very core of our hearts." Barclay, *The Gospel of John,* vol. 1, p. 224.

to it?" But Jesus, conscious that His disciples grumbled at this, said to them, "Does this cause you to stumble? What then if you should behold the Son of Man ascending where He was before? It is the Spirit who gives life; the flesh profits nothing; the words that I have spoken to you are spirit and are life. But there are some of you who do not believe." For Jesus knew from the beginning who they were who did not believe, and who it was that would betray Him. And He was saying, "For this reason I have said to you, that no one can come to Me, unless it has been granted him from the Father."

As a result of this many of His disciples withdrew, and were not walking with Him anymore. (vv. 60–66)

Clearly, the followers described in these verses are unbelievers (vv. 63–64) who found Christ's words difficult to choke down (v. 60).[3]

B. Firm determination. Simon Peter exemplifies the second type of follower.

Jesus said therefore to the twelve, "You do not want to go away also, do you?" Simon Peter answered Him, "Lord, to whom shall we go? You have words of eternal life. And we have believed and have come to know that You are the Holy One of God." (vv. 67–69)

The thinning crowds did nothing to thin the determination of Christ's closest disciples. Rather, their resolve became firmer than ever.

C. Subtle deception. Standing right in the midst of the chosen band of men was one who looked and sounded like the most sincere disciple. His name was Judas, a name which has itself become a metaphor for betrayal.

Jesus answered them, "Did I Myself not choose you, the twelve, and yet one of you is a devil?" Now He meant Judas the son of Simon Iscariot, for he, one of the twelve, was going to betray Him. (vv. 70–71)

Which category do you fall into? Is your life like the grumbling crowd—one of open defection? Or is your life like Judas—

---

3. *Difficult* here means not so much that the saying is vague or hard to understand but that it is hard to accept. The Greek word is *sklēros*, meaning "hard to the touch, rough." It is used in James 3:4, speaking of "strong winds," and also in Jude 15 to describe "harsh things" that were spoken.

one of subtle deception? Or is it like Peter and the other disciples—one of firm determination?

A Concluding Application

As long as Jesus is merely a figure in a book, He remains outside of us. But when we invite Him to enter our hearts, we can feed upon His life and be sustained by the very source of life Himself. William Barclay makes a clarifying comparison:

Think of it this way. Here in a bookcase is a book which a man has never read. It may be the glory and the wonder of the tragedies of Shakespeare; but so long as it remains unread upon his bookshelves it is external to him. One day he takes it down and reads it. He is thrilled and fascinated and moved. The story sticks to him; the great lines remain in his memory; now when he wants to, he can take that wonder out from inside himself and remember it and think about it and feed his mind and his heart upon it. Once the book was outside him. Now it is inside him and he can feed upon it.[4]

If you've never taken Jesus into your life, assimilated His being into yours, then He is outside of your life. As with a child whose nose is pressed against a bakery store window, it doesn't matter how close you are to the bread or how sweet or fresh you think its smell is. If you don't reach out and take Him as the Bread of Life, then He's forever encased on the shelf, while you're forever on the street—hungry.

Living Insights

In Jesus, God satisfies the hungry soul with the gift of "the finest of the wheat" (Ps. 81:16). Jesus is the Bread that nourishes us unto eternal life—if we'll but receive the Father's gift.

Eternal life, the triumphing over death, is granted as a grace of God. It's about Him, not us, as Paul wrote in Ephesians:

4. Barclay, *The Gospel of John*, vol. 1, p. 224.

Immense in mercy and with an incredible love, [God] embraced us. He took our sin-dead lives and made us alive in Christ. He did all this on his own, with no help from us! Then he picked us up and set us down in highest heaven in company with Jesus, our Messiah.

Now God has us where he wants us, with all the time in this world and the next to shower grace and kindness upon us in Christ Jesus. Saving is all his idea, and all his work. All we do is trust him enough to let him do it. It's God's gift from start to finish! We don't play the major role. If we did, we'd probably go around bragging that we'd done the whole thing! No, we neither make nor save ourselves. God does both the making and saving.[5] (2:4–9)

Have you accepted God's gift to you? There is no other Bread by which we can be nourished. There is no other way for us to enter into eternal life. Being a good person doesn't cut it—we're still stained with sin, every one of us helplessly fallen short of God's glory (Rom. 3:23). In our sin-hobbled state, no matter how hard we try to break free from our human limitations, we're still bound and pulled toward death (6:23a). That's not the Lord's desire for us, though: "The free gift of God is eternal life in Christ Jesus our Lord" (v. 23b).

Accept God's provision, won't you? Right now, right where you are, confess your need for Him and tell Him how grateful you are to accept His gift of Jesus Christ as your Savior. Tell Him that you're putting your faith in Him and no more in yourself. Then let Him welcome you into His family, for now you are His very own child (John 1:12–13; 1 John 3:1–2).

5. Eugene H. Peterson, *The Message: The New Testament in Contemporary English* (Colorado Springs, Colo.: NavPress, 1993), p. 403.

Charting the Bread of Life Discourse in John 6

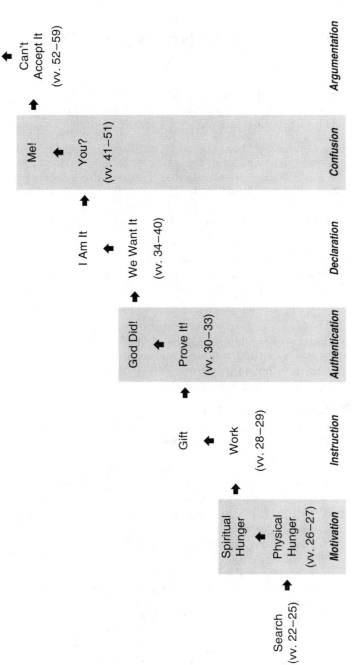

You Have
No Life

Can't
Accept It
(vv. 52–59)

Me!   You?
(vv. 41–51)

I Am It   We Want It
(vv. 34–40)

God Did!   Prove It!
(vv. 30–33)

Gift   Work
(vv. 28–29)

Spiritual   Physical
Hunger   Hunger
(vv. 26–27)

Search
(vv. 22–25)

Argumentation   *Confusion*   *Declaration*   *Authentication*   *Instruction*   *Motivation*

17

Chapter 3

Jesus in the Lions' Den

John 7

As classic as a Shakespearean drama and as edge-of-your-seat exciting as a Spielberg movie, the story of Daniel and the lions' den has captivated both young and old for generations.

Even if you haven't read the story in years, you probably still recall it with Technicolor vividness on your mental screen. The protagonist, ninety-year-old Daniel, was framed by a few jealous men in the king's court. Though innocent and faithful, he was thrown into a den of hungry lions. Waiting for the outcome was nerve-shattering: would he be ripped to shreds by the wild lions or would someone, somehow, come to his rescue?

Well, the king, who greatly respected Daniel, couldn't stand the suspense and came to the lions' den early the next morning. To his amazement, Daniel was still alive! God had rescued him, miraculously closing the lions' mouths.

Daniel was not the only one thrown to the lions. Jesus spent the last six months of His life in a lions' den of savages intent on tearing Him to pieces. Eventually these brutal animals cornered Him at the cross (Ps. 22:13). But in our study today, Jesus escapes the enemies' sharp fangs and manages to shut their objecting mouths.

I. Background and Setting

Before we lower ourselves into the lions' den with Jesus and His adversaries, let's get a good look at the scene in its geographic and cultural context.

   A. Where? Chapter 7 contains two lions' dens. The first is in Galilee (vv. 1–9), the quiet, safe, familiar home base of Jesus. The other is in Judea (vv. 10–52).

   B. Why? With the ill winds of hatred stirring up a storm of opposition against Jesus, talk of assassination swirls in the air. It's becoming dangerous for Jesus to be seen in Judea (v. 1), and His appearance at the Feast of Tabernacles, or Booths, in Jerusalem must be carefully arranged.

   C. When? Bible scholars generally agree that the time setting falls within the last six months of Jesus' life. Verse 2 cues us as to the specific time: "the feast of the Jews, the Feast of the Booths, was at hand." Israel celebrated three great annual feasts: Passover, Pentecost, and Tabernacles. The last was held in early October. It was a feast of thanksgiving primarily for the blessings of God in the harvest, but it was also a time of remembering the blessings received during the wilderness wanderings, the time when God dwelt with His people in the tabernacle (see Lev. 23:33–44). All Jewish males within a twenty-mile radius of Jerusalem were obligated to participate in this festive event, while a multitude of devout Jews from outside the area also attended.

II. People and Reactions

Like Daniel, the Lamb of God finds Himself surrounded by lions—fierce, savage beasts in human form who attack Him intensely and incessantly. This hostile attitude is seen first in His own brothers, then in the Jewish people, and ultimately in the crowd in general, who, for the most part, reject Him and His message.

A. His brothers. In verses 3–9, the roaring lions are Jesus' own brothers: James, Joseph, Simon, and Judas (compare Matt. 13:55).

> His brothers therefore said to Him, "Depart from here, and go into Judea, that Your disciples also may behold Your works which You are doing. For no one does anything in secret, when he himself seeks to be known publicly. If You do these things, show Yourself to the world." For not even His brothers were believing in Him.[1] (John 7:3–5)

"Hey, bro, if you're such a star, what are you doing here? You should be in Hollywood!" But Jesus responds to their sarcasm with seriousness.

> "My time is not yet at hand, but your time is always opportune. The world cannot hate you; but it hates Me because I testify of it, that its deeds are evil. Go up to the feast yourselves; I do not go up to this feast because My time has not yet fully come." And having said these things to them, He stayed in Galilee. (vv. 6–9)

When Jesus says "My time is not yet at hand," He uses a word that means "season."[2] It is commonly used to refer to the "harvest season" or the "time for figs." The time to reveal Himself is still too green. He must wait till the time is ripe.

---

1. The imperfect tense—"were believing"—indicates a continuing attitude.

2. Greek has two words for time: *chronos* and *kairos*. The one used in John 7:6 is *kairos*. Often, it "refers to time not simply in its chronological sequence, but with reference to the events that take place in it. Used in this way, it is time in its qualitative rather than its quantitative aspect. It points to the suitable time, the right time, the favorable opportunity." Leon Morris, *The Gospel according to John*, rev. ed., The New International Commentary on the New Testament Series (Grand Rapids, Mich.: William B. Eerdmans Publishing Co., 1995), pp. 351–52.

B. The Jews. In quiet, unpretentious obscurity, Jesus departs for the feast after His brothers have left (v. 10). But like the most suspenseful of spy novels, the plot thickens as the religious officials try to track Jesus down (v. 11). Finally, during the middle of the feast, Jesus makes His identity and whereabouts public—a courageous act in light of the fact that He's a target for assassination.

> But when it was now the midst of the feast Jesus went up into the temple, and began to teach. The Jews therefore were marveling, saying, "How has this man become learned, having never been educated?" (vv. 14–15)

The Jewish officials are most concerned about Jesus' credentials. "After all," they must have muttered among themselves, "the guy doesn't even have a seminary degree." They hold an arrogant contempt for this homespun, self-taught storyteller, but His lack of credentials should not be grounds for their dismissal of what He has to say. As commentator William Barclay notes:

> What right had this man to come and lay down the law? Jesus had no cultural background; he had no training in the rabbinic schools and colleges. Surely no intelligent person was going to listen to him? Here was the reaction of academic snobbery.
>
> Many of the greatest poets and writers and evangelists have had no technical qualifications at all. That is not for one moment to say that study and culture and education are to be despised and abandoned; but we must have a care never to wave a man away and consign him to the company who do not matter simply because he lacks the technical equipment of the schools.[3]

C. The crowd. Not only do the skeptical and antagonistic Jewish officials spot Jesus, the masses also see Him. And in spite of the overwhelmingly negative reviews of the critics, the multitudes make up their own minds about Him. But this new star, Jesus, doesn't open to rave reviews from them either. Their reaction is mixed (v. 12). Many people are paranoid, as we see in verse 20.

> The multitude answered, "You have a demon! Who seeks to kill You?"

---

3. William Barclay, *The Gospel of John,* rev. ed., The Daily Study Bible Series (Philadelphia, Pa.: Westminster Press, 1975), vol. 1, p. 234.

But some have a more courageous attitude (vv. 25–26), and others even believe.

> But many of the multitude believed in Him; and they were saying, "When the Christ shall come, He will not perform more signs than those which this man has, will He?" . . . Others were saying, "This is the Christ." (vv. 31, 41a)

Because of the diverse opinions about Jesus, tension charges the atmosphere.

> So there arose a division in the multitude because of Him. And some of them wanted to seize Him, but no one laid hands on Him. (vv. 43–44)

Although the Jewish officials are ready to pounce, they're held at bay—a mute testimony to the fact that there's no lion, even of the human variety, that God cannot tame.

III. Jesus and God

Let's focus the spotlight on the lion tamer and how He shuts the mouths of the ravenous beasts that surround Him.

A. The Father. With whip and chair, Jesus stands His ground calmly, with confidence and control—because the ground He stands on is shared with His heavenly Father (vv. 16–18, 33–34).

B. The Spirit. On the last day of the feast, Jesus makes a dramatic statement about Himself (vv. 37–38). But to appreciate the drama of the event, you must understand a little of the ceremonial background to that final day.

> Each day of the festival the people came with their palms and their willows to the Temple; with them they formed a kind of screen or roof and marched round the great altar. At the same time a priest took a golden pitcher . . . and went down to the Pool of Siloam and filled it with water. It was carried back through the Water Gate while the people recited Isaiah 12:3: "With joy you will draw water from the wells of salvation." The water was carried up to the Temple altar and poured out as an offering to God. . . . The whole dramatic ceremony was a vivid thanksgiving for God's good gift of water and an acted prayer for rain, and a memory of the water which sprang from the rock when they travelled through the wilderness.[4]

4. Barclay, *The Gospel of John,* vol. 1, p. 249.

Against this background, the time is ripe for Jesus to reveal His identity. Dramatically, He stands and shouts:

> "If any man is thirsty, let him come to Me and drink. He who believes in Me, as the Scripture said, 'From his innermost being shall flow rivers of living water.'" (vv. 37b–38)

Even knowing that He is opening Himself to attack, Jesus shows His concern for these people's lives. He not only stands up, making Himself an easy target, but He extends His hand to these ruthless lions, offering their lashing tongues the refreshing water of the Holy Spirit.

A Lion That Spoke Up

In the peripheral shadows of that lions' den, a voice speaks up in defense of Jesus.

> Nicodemus said to them (he who came to Him before, being one of them), "Our Law does not judge a man, unless it first hears from him and knows what he is doing, does it?" (vv. 50–51)

Remember Nicodemus from chapter 3, the Jewish leader who came to Jesus concealed by night? Here we see him take a tentative but definite step out into the open. Finally, by the end of the Gospel, Nicodemus will boldly identify himself with Christ. He, along with Joseph of Arimathea, will take Jesus' ravaged body from the cross and give the Savior a quiet, tender burial (19:38–42).

Little by little, Nicodemus' faith grew, and eventually he came forward . . . in an act of love for the Savior, who loved him so patiently and accepted him so readily even though he stood at a distance in the shadows.

Isn't it time you came out of the shadows? Isn't it time you separated from the pack and stepped forward publicly to identify yourself with Jesus? He is calling with outstretched arms: "If any man is thirsty, let him come to Me and drink."

Living Insights

There's certainly one thing Jesus teaches us: God does not do what we expect. He has His own plans, His own timing, His own methods. And He is definitely not limited by our limited understanding of His Book. Let's comb back through John 7 to see what the expectations were, what happened when they weren't met, and what Jesus' purpose was.

What did Jesus' brothers expect of Him in verses 2–4? What did they think He wanted to be?

_____

_____

How does Jesus' response to them in verses 6–8 counter their expectations? Would you have expected Him to say what He did in verse 7? Is this your picture of Jesus?

_____

_____

_____

What was the expectation of the Jews in verse 15? Does this color your willingness to accept what certain teachers and authors have to say? Is this a reliable measure? Why or why not?

_____

_____

_____

How does Jesus' response in verses 16–19 and 21–24 challenge their reaction to Him?

_____

_____

_____

In verses 27, 41b–42, 52, what were the expectations of the people? They weren't being merely good students of prophecy and Scripture, were they? There's presumption here—what were they presuming?

_____

_____

_____

How does Jesus' response in verses 28–29 and 33–34 challenge their assumptions? What is He trying to tell them?

_____

_____

_____

_____

What is the result of the Jewish officials, Jesus' brothers, and some of the crowd not having their expectations met (vv. 1, 3–5, 11, 13, 25, 30, 32b, 44, 49)?

_____

_____

_____

How do Jesus' words in verses 37–38 challenge the attitude of His enemies' hearts?

_____

_____

_____

Commentator Lesslie Newbigin crystallizes the tensions in John 7 for us and leaves us with a memorable lesson:

> [Jesus] gives life; they want to kill. This is what happens, and will always happen, when the attempt is made to capture the revelation of God and make it a possession of men.[5]

---

5. Lesslie Newbigin, _The Light Has Come: An Exposition of the Fourth Gospel_ (Grand Rapids, Mich.: William B. Eerdmans Publishing Co., 1982), p. 96.

Chapter 4

Letters in the Sand

John 8:1–11

It started with a look . . . an innocent look, without premeditation or evil intent. But it was a short, slippery step from a look to lust, from infatuation to infidelity. Because the look eventually led to a touch. The touch then led to a kiss. And that kiss led to the forbidden intimacy of adultery.

Where did the adultery lead? Not to secret satisfaction (which never lasts anyway), but to public humiliation. Not to a softly-lit afterglow, but to a glaring, potentially fatal aftermath.

Are we talking about a fatal attraction? The rage of a jealous or spurned lover? No, John 8 pictures for us the self-proclaimed guardians of righteousness setting up a sinful rendezvous to spring a trap.

Not to catch the lovers, necessarily. In fact, they use only one of the lovers, the woman, whose tangled life they hope will ensnarl the one they're after. The Pharisees, you see, are after bigger game, the One who breaks their Sabbath with healings and claims to come from God. Jesus is their quarry, and this poor lost woman is only their means to string Him up.

I. The Setting
The setting is established for us in verses 1–2.
> But Jesus went to the Mount of Olives. And early in the morning He came again into the temple, and all the people were coming to Him; and He sat down and began to teach them.

The morning is like any other Jerusalem morning. It is early; the city is still damp with dew as purple shadows fall among the temple columns. Echoing through the temple are the words of Jesus, who, in rabbinical fashion, sits down to teach the gathered people.

II. The Attack
Suddenly, the serenity of that sacred place is shattered.
A. The interruption.
> And the scribes and the Pharisees brought a woman caught in adultery. (v. 3a)

The scribes and Pharisees, Israel's supposed spokesmen for God, are bent on destroying Jesus, who poses a threat to their religious oligarchy. Jesus stops teaching; He stares at the men whose voices have been honed on hate. A quick glance at verse 6 reveals that they're acting out a plot that has been rehearsed down to the last detail—a plot so insidious that they are willing to entrap and execute a woman in order to discredit Jesus.

B. The accusation. With them they drag, like a squirming dog on a leash, a disheveled woman, hastily clothed, barefooted, and humiliated. A woman, they testify, caught in "the very act" of adultery (v. 4). A woman taken abruptly from the bedroom, where she was some man's sexual object, and insensitively dragged to the temple, where she now becomes a political object used to bait the trap set for Jesus.

Dehumanizing People

When we treat people as things, we dehumanize them and destroy something precious inside them. The scribes and Pharisees were not looking at this woman as a person but as a thing—an instrument whereby they could formulate a charge against Jesus. They were using her as a man might use a worthless pawn in a chess game. To them, she had no name, no personality, no heart, no feelings, no soul. She was simply an expendable pawn in their strategy to corner Jesus into a checkmate.

Whether you use people for your own pleasure or to prove your point, even a religious point, you are treating those people as things to be used instead of human beings to be loved. And this greatly dishonors the One in whose image they were made.

C. The question. They set the trap with hair-trigger precision:

"Now in the Law Moses commanded us to stone
such women; what then do You say?"[1] (v. 5)

Judaism's three gravest crimes—idolatry, murder, and adultery —were all punishable by death.

The *Mishnah,* that is, the Jewish codified law, states that the penalty for adultery is strangulation, and even the method of strangulation is laid down. "The man is to be enclosed in dung up to his knees, and a soft towel set within a rough towel is to be placed around his neck (in order that no mark may be

---

1. The Greek text helps capture the emphasis by putting the personal pronoun at the beginning of the sentence. The sense is "*You* now, what's *your* advice?" Clearly, they were trying to place the problem squarely on Jesus.

made, for the punishment is God's punishment). Then one man draws in one direction and another in the other direction, until he be dead." The *Mishnah* reiterates that death by stoning is the penalty for a girl who is betrothed and who then commits adultery.[2]

Furthermore, Moses wrote that if the offense took place in a city, both adulterers were to be stoned publicly (Deut. 22:22–24). So the Pharisees' appeal in John 8:5 to the Law of Moses raises an important question: Where is the guilty man? The accusers testify that the woman was caught "in the very act," so certainly they had equal opportunity to apprehend the man as well. As the pieces of this sordid puzzle begin to fall in place, it seems likely that the scribes and Pharisees did not merely happen by the bedroom window of these clandestine lovers. No, the incident smacks suspiciously of a premeditated trap. Before they could land their trophy fish, they had to first dip their minnow net into the shallows to get their bait. Having caught her, they now hope to hook Christ on the barbs of a dilemma. If He says, "Yes, stone her," His compassion for people will be questioned and He will place Himself in jeopardy with the Romans, since the Roman government retained the right to exercise capital punishment. However, if He says, "No, release her," He will be accused of not supporting the Law of Moses, thus alienating Himself from the Jews. Essentially, the Pharisees are asking: "What will it be, Jesus? Do you kill the woman or kill the Law?"

III. The Answer

Between this rock and hard place, Jesus stands firm, refusing to compromise either His principles or the person for whom those principles were given.

A. To the men.

And they were saying this, testing Him, in order that they might have grounds for accusing Him. But Jesus stooped down, and with His finger wrote on the ground. But when they persisted in asking Him, He straightened up, and said to them, "He who is without sin among you, let him be the first to throw a stone at her." And again He stooped down, and wrote on the ground. And when they heard it, they began to go out one by one, beginning with the

2. William Barclay, *The Gospel of John*, rev. ed., The Daily Study Bible Series (Philadelphia, Pa.: Westminster Press, 1975), vol. 2, p. 2.

older ones, and He was left alone, and the woman,
where she had been, in the midst. (John 8:6–9)

What Jesus writes in the sand remains a mystery to this day
(v. 6b),[3] but what He says to this self-righteous, self-appointed
judge and jury has echoed throughout the centuries. Deuter-
onomy 17:7 declared that the witnesses were to be the first
to stone the victim, so Jesus merely forces these legalists to
go strictly by the Law. He makes only one qualification: that
they take a look at the log in their own eyes before they try
to take the speck out of somebody else's (Matt. 7:1–5).

B. To the woman. As if an angel has passed between the helpless
woman and the mob, there is silence; then the vigilantes re-
treat home, heads hung in shame—or, at least, in defeat. What
a contrast she and Jesus make: the guilty and the guiltless,
adulteress and advocate, sinner and Savior.

And straightening up, Jesus said to her, "Woman,
where are they? Did no one condemn you?" And
she said, "No one, Lord." (vv. 10–11a)

IV. The Counsel

Demonstrating that He is truly "full of grace and truth" (1:14), Jesus
forgives the sinner without condoning the sin.

And Jesus said, "Neither do I condemn you; go your way.
From now on sin no more." (8:11b)

He cares—"neither do I condemn you"; and He confronts—"sin
no more." Undoubtedly, this has been the darkest moment of this
woman's life, until the Light of the World bathes her sin in the
radiance of His forgiving presence (12:46). The only One supremely
qualified to condemn her, doesn't (v. 47).

V. The Principles

From this passage, three truths emerge that we can apply in our
relationships today.

**A. The practice of confronting wrong calls for humility, not
pride.** Jesus exhorts us in the Sermon on the Mount to look
closely at our own lives before we look critically at the lives
of others (Matt. 7:5). Paul echoes this in Galatians 6:1:

Brethren, even if a man is caught in any trespass,
you who are spiritual, restore such a one in a spirit
of gentleness; each one looking to yourself, lest you
too be tempted.

---

3. The Greek term used here is not the word normally used for *writing* in the New Testament—
graphō. Rather, it is the word *katagraphō*. Some commentators suggest that Jesus may be listing
in the sand the sins of the scribes and Pharisees in order to prick their consciences (compare
Job 13:26).

None of us is exempt from stumbling into sin, as Eugene Peterson reiterates in his paraphrase of Paul's words: "*You* might be needing forgiveness before the day's out."[4] If we take the least glimmer of satisfaction in confronting someone else about their sin, that is an indication of pride. We need to nip that in the bud, or we will live to see it grow to overrun our lives.

B. **The privilege of condemning wrong is based on righteousness, not knowledge.** Are you "without sin" so that you feel free to cast the first stone (John 8:7)? Are your eyes without logs so that you can see to take the specks out of the eyes of others (Matt. 7:5)? Are you spiritual enough to restore the one caught in a trespass (Gal. 6:1)? If you're not, then don't (Matt. 7:1–2).

C. **The principle of correcting wrong starts with forgiveness, not rebuke.** Notice the pattern in the way Jesus deals with the guilty woman: "Neither do I condemn you; go your way. From now on sin no more" (John 8:11). Can you imagine a world free from condemnation and judging . . . a world marked by forgiveness, not perfection? Just as the journey of a thousand miles begins with the first step, so the task of a world free from judging begins with one person willing to take the first step of compassion and forgiveness. Won't you be that person?

Living Insights

It's easy with a story like this in John 8 to feel superior to the Pharisees. But are we really so different from them?

Suppose, for a moment, that the woman in the story wasn't an adulteress. Suppose that she was a lesbian or a woman who had had an abortion or a drunk driver or a prostitute. That can put the pharisaical shoe on the other foot, can't it?

If one of these possibilities had been the scenario in John 8, would that change your attitude toward the Pharisees, toward the woman, or toward Christ? If so, how? And why?

_____

_____

_____

4. Eugene H. Peterson, *The Message: The New Testament in Contemporary English* (Colorado Springs, Colo.: NavPress, 1993), p. 399.

_____

_____

_____

Sometimes, with particular sins, we Christians are a little more reluctant to drop our stones, a little more ready to condemn, and a lot less glad to hear Jesus say, "Neither do I condemn you." Jesus, though, who takes sin much more seriously than we do,

> responds to it differently from what most of us are used to. He does not condemn, rejecting the repentant sinner; He does not condone, ignoring the sin; He forgives.[5]

Why did the Pharisees resist God's forgiveness? Why do we sometimes resist God's forgiveness?

_____

_____

_____

_____

_____

Why do we so easily judge others? What does James have to say about this tendency (see James 4:11–12)?

_____

_____

_____

_____

How does Jesus want us to handle situations where others have sinned, according to . . .

Matthew 7:12 _____

_____

_____

5. Eugene H. Peterson, _Forces Concealed in Quiet: Meditations from the Writings of John the Apostle_ (Nashville, Tenn.: Thomas Nelson Publishers, 1985), no. 70.

Matthew 18:15 _____

_____

_____

Romans 14:13, 19 _____

_____

_____

Galatians 6:1–5 _____

_____

_____

1 Peter 4:8 _____

_____

_____

Jesus' goal is not to judge and condemn but to save and restore (compare 1 Tim. 1:15–17). Yes, He tells the truth about our world, that "its deeds are evil" (John 7:7). He's honest about our darkness, but He comes to light our way to life (8:12). As Paul wrote,

> Do you not know that the unrighteous shall not inherit the kingdom of God: Do not be deceived; neither fornicators, nor idolaters, nor adulterers, nor effeminate, nor homosexuals, nor thieves, nor the covetous, nor drunkards, nor revilers, nor swindlers, shall inherit the kingdom of God. *And such were some of you; but you were washed, but you were sanctified, but you were justified in the name of the Lord Jesus Christ, and in the Spirit of our God.* (1 Cor. 6:9–11, emphasis added)

Righteousness is a gift—for *all* of us (Rom. 3:21–27a). So let's spend our time praising God for His mercy instead of passing sentence on others.

Chapter 5
Reasons for Rejection
John 8:12–59

Dwight L. Moody, by his own admission, made a mistake on the eighth of October 1871—a mistake he determined never to repeat.

He had been preaching in the city of Chicago. That particular night drew his largest audience yet. His message was "What will you do then with Jesus who is called the Christ?"

By the end of the service, he was tired. He concluded his message with a presentation of the gospel and a concluding statement: "Now I give you a week to think that over. And when we come together again, you will have opportunity to respond."

A soloist began to sing. But before the final note, the music was drowned out by clanging bells and wailing sirens screaming through the streets. The great Chicago Fire was blazing. In the ashen aftermath, hundreds were dead and over a hundred thousand were homeless.

Quite possibly, some who heard Moody's message that night would die in the fire that would rage for the next two days. He reflected remorsefully that he would never again give an audience another week to think over the message of the gospel.

If you were a victim of a fire like that, would you know with certainty whether you would spend eternity with Christ in heaven? Not *hope* or *wish* or *pray* that you would go there—but *know*?

If not, this chapter will allow you the opportunity to gain that confidence as we listen in on a debate about the Person of Christ and hear His remarkable claims firsthand.

I. The Background and Setting
The background to our passage is the Jewish Feast of Tabernacles (John 7:2), an annual festival of feasting and religious ceremony. The time, apparently, is the day after the final day of the festival (vv. 37, 53). The setting is the temple treasury (8:20), which was located near the Court of the Women (so named because women could enter this part of the temple too). On the first evening of the Feast of Tabernacles,

> there was a ceremony called The Illumination of the Temple. It took place in the Court of the Women. . . . When the dark came . . . four great candelabra were lit

and, it was said, they sent such a blaze of light throughout Jerusalem that every courtyard was lit up with their
brilliance.[1]
This magnificent light was a reminder of God's pillar of fire that
guided and protected Israel through the wilderness. The candela-
bra were probably extinguished on the last day of the Feast,[2] providing a strong visual backdrop for Jesus' next amazing claim.

II. Declaration and Response
The verbal sword fight between Jesus and the Pharisees begins in
verses 12–13.

A. The radical testimony of Jesus. In verse 12, Jesus begins the
fencing match.

> "I am the light of the world; he who follows Me shall
> not walk in the darkness, but shall have the light
> of life."

The claim is exclusive, one only God could make. And it is
especially poignant coming after the great light in the temple
had so recently been put out. Note that Jesus claimed to be *the*
Light of the World, not *a* light. Although the claim is *ex*clusive,
the offer is *in*clusive—an offer any and all could respond to.

B. The rapier thrust of the Pharisees. Responding to the bold
claims of Jesus, the Pharisees lash back with a sharp retort.
The fencing match is under way.

> "You are bearing witness of Yourself; Your witness
> is not true." (v. 13)

III. Discussion and Debate
Following the initial clash of swords, words fly back and forth in
unsheathed passion.

A. General attitudes. The attitude of the Pharisees progressively
and heatedly escalates from contradiction (v. 13) to insinuation (v. 19) to denial (v. 33) to insult (v. 48) to sarcasm (v. 53)
and, finally and climactically, to violence (v. 59).

B. Specific reasons. Threaded within the fabric of these verses
are five specific reasons why the Pharisees rejected the Savior
and His words.

1. Lack of knowledge. Perhaps the most universal reason for
rejecting Jesus is ignorance—an ignorance these Pharisees, along with their ancestors (see Hos. 4:1–3, 6),
clearly demonstrate.

---

1. William Barclay, *The Gospel of John,* rev. ed., The Daily Study Bible Series (Philadelphia, Pa.:
Westminster Press, 1975), vol. 2, p. 11.

2. Merrill C. Tenney, "The Gospel of John," *The Expositor's Bible Commentary,* gen. ed. Frank E.
Gaebelein (Grand Rapids, Mich.: Zondervan Publishing House, 1981), vol. 9, p. 92.

> Jesus answered and said to them, "Even if I bear
> witness of Myself, My witness is true; for I know
> where I came from, and where I am going; but
> you do not know where I come from, or where
> I am going." . . . And so they were saying to
> Him, "Where is Your Father?" Jesus answered,
> "You know neither Me, nor My Father; if you
> knew Me, you would know My Father also."
> (John 8:14, 19)

Despite the evidence of Jesus' miracles of healing and
feeding and His message of truth and grace, the Pharisees
don't—or won't—perceive who He is. And because they
don't recognize Him, they don't recognize the One He
represents—who is the One whose children *they* claim to
be! But the God they seem to have made for themselves
is a hard, mean, tyrant of a God; so they expect their
Messiah to be "tough on sinners" too. Somehow, in all
their scriptural expertise, they missed God's own description of Himself:

> "The Lord, the Lord God, compassionate and
> gracious, slow to anger, and abounding in
> lovingkindness and truth; who keeps loving-
> kindness for thousands, who forgives iniquity,
> transgression and sin." (Exod. 34:6–7a; see
> also Num. 14:18a; Neh. 9:17; Ps. 86:15; 103;
> Joel 2:13)

And in all their study of God's Law, they surely seemed
to miss the heart of it: "You shall love your neighbor as
yourself; I am the Lord" (Lev. 19:18b).

2. **Lack of perception.** The Pharisees' lack of perception is
brought into focus in verses 15 and 23. Verse 15 highlights
their problem, while verse 23 explains why they have it.
The problem: "You people judge according to the flesh"
(v. 15a). They draw their conclusions from the wrong
standard. Looking to externals, they see Jesus only as
Joseph's son, the carpenter. They don't have the discernment to see beneath the flesh and blood into the spiritual
dimension. The cause: "You are from below . . . you are
of this world" (v. 23). Because they have not been born
again (3:3), their frame of reference is horizontal rather
than vertical (compare Isa. 55:8–9). The inevitable result
of such nearsightedness is found in John 8:24.

> "Unless you believe that I am He, you shall die
> in your sins."

3. **Lack of appropriation.** Since "faith comes from hearing, and hearing by the word of Christ" (Rom. 10:17), the seed of God's Word plays an essential role in our hearts. There can be no fruit without growth, no growth without life, and no life without a seed. And it is at these Pharisees' fallow hearts that Jesus points His finger.

> "I know that you are Abraham's offspring; yet you seek to kill Me, because My word has no place in you. . . . Why do you not understand what I am saying? It is because you cannot hear My word." (John 8:37, 43)

Remember, now, the Pharisees have majored in religion; they are professionals. Descendants of the great patriarch Abraham, they're also the resident textual and theological experts. But, as John establishes early in his Gospel, we are born into God's family as one of His children, "not of blood, nor of the will of the flesh, nor of the will of man, but of God" (1:13). We become His children by personally receiving Him (v. 12)—not by pedigree, proximity, or credentials.

4. **Lack of desire.** In chapter 8, verses 44 and 45, Jesus lunges His sword into the Pharisees' hearts.

> "You are of your father the devil, and you want to do the desires of your father. He was a murderer from the beginning, and does not stand in the truth, because there is no truth in him. Whenever he speaks a lie, he speaks from his own nature; for he is a liar, and the father of lies. But because I speak the truth, you do not believe Me."

Although the Jewish officials could trace their lineage back to Abraham, their spiritual lineage goes all the way back to the Devil himself. The Serpent of old had enticed them away from the true God with the seductive apple of religiosity. But under the Devil's clerical garb, he is both a murderer and a liar. And, like father, like son, the Pharisees were a mirrored reflection, twisting the truth about Jesus (v. 48) and plotting to kill Him (v. 40).

5. **Lack of humility.** In response to Jesus' piercing words, the Pharisees strike back with the worst slurs they can think of.

> "Do we not say rightly that You are a Samaritan and have a demon?" (v. 48)

To not lend any credence to their prejudice, Jesus does not even respond to their calling Him a Samaritan. He does, however, castigate them for profaning what is holy.

> Jesus answered, "I do not have a demon; but I honor My Father, and you dishonor Me. But I do not seek My glory; there is One who seeks and judges. Truly, truly, I say to you, if anyone keeps My word he shall never see death."[3] (vv. 49–51)

To defend themselves against Jesus' sword of truth, the Pharisees lunge at Him with the broadsword of pride.

> The Jews said to Him, "Now we know that You have a demon. Abraham died, and the prophets also; and You say, 'If anyone keeps My word, he shall never taste of death.' Surely You are not greater than our father Abraham, who died? The prophets died too; whom do You make Yourself out to be?" (vv. 52–53)

"Who do You think You are!" they shout at Jesus, "someone greater than *our* father Abraham?" Previously, they had thrust a nasty insinuation at Jesus: "Where is *Your* Father?" (v. 19). And they followed that up with an even uglier innuendo: "We were not born of fornication" (v. 41). But their pride was about to take a startling fall.

IV. Violence and Escape

Appealing to their family tree, Jesus uses the physical parentage of the Pharisees to His advantage.

---

3. Jesus "is not suggesting that his disciples will never experience physical dissolution. Rather, they will never have to confront death in its terror as the occasion of final separation from God; death as the curse of sin." Bruce Milne, *The Message of John: Here Is Your King!*, The Bible Speaks Today Series (Downers Grove, Ill.: InterVarsity Press, 1993), p. 135.

"Your father Abraham rejoiced to see My day, and he saw it and was glad." The Jews therefore said to Him, "You are not yet fifty years old, and have You seen Abraham?" Jesus said to them, "Truly, truly, I say to you, before Abraham was born, I am." (vv. 56–58)

Earlier in this Gospel, we saw Jesus claiming "I am the bread of life" (6:48) and "I am the light of the world" (8:12). In 8:58, He says simply, yet dramatically, "I am." In doing so, Jesus claims not only timeless existence but also equality with the God of the Old Testament (compare Exod. 3:14). To the Pharisees, this is blasphemy—a sin that, like adultery, carries the penalty of stoning.

Therefore they picked up stones to throw at Him; but Jesus hid Himself, and went out of the temple. (John 8:59)

A Final Application

We may either cast stones at Jesus, like the Pharisees, or throw ourselves at His feet, accepting Him as our Lord and Savior. C. S. Lewis brings the choice into clear focus.

'What are we to make of Christ?' . . . You must accept or reject the story.

The things He says are very different from what any other teacher has said. Others say, 'This is the truth about the Universe. This is the way you ought to go,' but He says, 'I am the Truth, and the Way, and the Life.' He says, 'No man can reach absolute reality, except through Me.'[4]

Which will it be? Your eternal destiny depends on whether you accept or reject His claims . . . whether you're clutching stones or clinging to the Savior.

Living Insights

We've traced the reasons for the Pharisees' rejection of Jesus; now let's give our attention to three promises that Jesus makes in this passage that offer the gift of life.

"I am the light of the world; he who follows Me shall not walk in the darkness, but shall have the light of life." (John 8:12)

---

4. C. S. Lewis, "What Are We to Make of Jesus Christ?" from *God in the Dock: Essays on Theology and Ethics*, ed. Walter Hooper (Grand Rapids, Mich.: William B. Eerdmans Publishing Co., 1970), p. 160.

"If you abide in My word, then you are truly disciples of Mine; and you shall know the truth, and the truth shall make you free." (vv. 31–32)

"Truly, truly, I say to you, if anyone keeps My word he shall never see death." (v. 51)

How do you think these three promises relate to each other? For example, what connections do you see between light and truth? Between Christ's light and freedom? Between the light of life and never seeing death?

_____

_____

_____

_____

_____

How do walking in darkness, being enslaved to sin (v. 34), and death connect with each other?

_____

_____

_____

_____

_____

Many times, our human idea of freedom doesn't match with God's. We usually take freedom to mean that we can do anything we want—whether it's moral or immoral. But when we choose a way that's opposite from God's way, we often wind up with painful consequences and regrets. We stumble around in the dark, get tangled up in sin, and distance ourselves from God—which is a taste of spiritual death.

This is not what Jesus, the Light of the World, wants for us. Let's explore for a moment the true freedom He offers us by understanding what He has freed us *from* and what He has freed us *for.*

Jesus Has Freed Us From . . .

Romans 5:9 _____

_____

Romans 6:22 _____

_____

Romans 8:1 _____

_____

1 Corinthians 29b, 31 _____

_____

Galatians 3:13 _____

_____

Ephesians 3:12; Hebrews 4:16 _____

_____

_____

Colossians 1:13; 1 John 4:4 _____

_____

_____

Jesus Has Freed Us For . . .

Matthew 25:31–40; 1 Corinthians 12:25 _____

_____

_____

Romans 6:18; 15:3; 2 Corinthians 5:21 _____

_____

_____

Romans 8:29; 12:2 _____

_____

Romans 12:4–5; Ephesians 4:16 _____

_____

_____

1 Corinthians 12:25 _____

_____

2 Corinthians 5:18–20 _____

_____

2 Corinthians 9:6–11; 1 Timothy 6:18 _____

_____

_____

1 Peter 4:2; 1 John 2:17 _____

_____

_____

Ultimately, life and freedom will be found in holiness and love (John 13:34–35; 1 Cor. 13; 1 Pet. 1:15), because these qualities emanate from the ultimate reality Himself.

Chapter 6
Blind Men's Bluff
John 9

At only nineteen-months old, after a severe illness, Helen Keller became blind, deaf, and, soon afterwards, unable to speak. Yet, through the patient work of one dedicated person, Helen was able to make a meaningful contribution to the world through her writing, teaching, and inspirational example. In one of her memoirs, Keller records endless days of anticipation and despair, waiting for someone to draw her out. Then she describes the day she first met the person who would do just that—lifelong friend and teacher, Anne Sullivan.

> Have you ever been at sea in a dense fog, when it seemed as if a tangible white darkness shut you in, and the great ship, tense and anxious, groped her way toward the shore with plummet and sounding-line, and you waited with beating heart for something to happen? I was like that ship before my education began, only I was without compass or sounding-line, and had no way of knowing how near the harbour was. "Light! give me light!" was the wordless cry of my soul, and the light of love shone on me in that very hour.
>
> I felt approaching footsteps. I stretched out my hand as I supposed to my mother. Someone took it, and I was caught up and held close in the arms of her who had come to reveal all things to me, and, more than all things else, to love me.[1]

This tender meeting between teacher and pupil on March 3, 1887, was the turning point of six-year-old Helen's life.

The blind man in John 9 had a similar encounter. For years he sat in the streets, a castaway from society, his soul aching for the touch of light and love. And then one day he heard the approaching footsteps of Jesus, who, with a touch of compassion, gave him new eyes.

I. Case and Cure
Few afflictions are more difficult to bear than blindness. And in Jesus' day, a blind person held little hope for anything more than a lifetime of begging. In the passage we're considering today, our Lord, the Light of the World, releases a blind man from the constraints of darkness. But because the healing is performed on the Jewish Sabbath, the Pharisees are critical. This leads to yet another

---

1. Helen Keller, *The Story of My Life* (Garden City, N.Y.: Doubleday and Co., 1905), p. 35.

public conflict between organized, legalistic religion and a vibrant, life-giving relationship with the person of Christ. Toward the end of the chapter it becomes clear that the real blind men are the Pharisees, whose spiritual darkness substitutes the pride of religion for the humility of faith.

A. **The man.** The focal point of chapter 9 rests on a beggar with congenital blindness (v. 1) . . . a man who has never seen the cresting sapphire waves of the Mediterranean surf; never seen the trees blossoming in spring; never seen the brilliant sunsets of the Palestinian plain; never seen the awe-inspiring architecture of the temple.

B. **The issue.** The theological issue is articulated this time not by the scribes and Pharisees but by Jesus' own disciples.

> And His disciples asked Him, saying, "Rabbi, who sinned, this man or his parents, that he should be born blind?" (v. 2)

Their question was logical. In those days, it was commonly taught that a fetus could commit sin while in the mother's womb and that its kicking indicated its sinful state. The Torah, the book of traditional Jewish laws, claimed that it was also possible for God to impose judgment of the parents' iniquity upon their children or grandchildren. We see this happen today when venereal diseases and alcoholism pass on birth defects to the next generation. Like medieval theologians who argued over how many angels could fit on the head of a pin, these fledgling seminarians were moved to theological controversy rather than tenderhearted compassion. But instead of scolding His students, Jesus gives them a short lecture on Christology.

> "It was neither that this man sinned, nor his parents; but it was in order that the works of God might be displayed in him. We must work the works of Him who sent Me, as long as it is day; night is coming, when no man can work. While I am in the world, I am the light of the world."[2] (vv. 3–5)

C. **The miracle.** The Bible records three times that Jesus used saliva to effect a miracle: in Mark 7:33 and 8:23, and here in verses 6–7 of John 9.

> When He had said this, He spat on the ground, and

---

2. "The healing of the blind man affirmed Jesus' identity as the Messiah, for the Old Testament predicted that the Messiah would come to heal the blind (Isaiah 29:18; 35:5; 42:7)." Bruce B. Barton, Philip W. Comfort, David R. Veerman, and Neil Wilson, *John*, Life Application Bible Commentary series (Wheaton, Ill.: Tyndale House Publishers, 1993), p. 194.

made clay of the spittle, and applied the clay to his eyes, and said to him, "Go, wash in the pool of Siloam" (which is translated, Sent). And so he went away and washed, and came back seeing.

Questions shoot up their hands and wave for an answer—Why clay? Why spittle? Why the pool of Siloam? But they are drowned out by the jubilation of the beggar returning from the pool, seeing for the first time in his life.

Some Personal Application

Helen Keller tells of the dramatic moment when Anne Sullivan first broke through her dark, silent world with the illumination of language.

> We walked down the path to the well-house, attracted by the fragrance of the honeysuckle with which it was covered. Some one was drawing water and my teacher placed my hand under the spout. As the cool stream gushed over one hand she spelled into the other the word *water*, first slowly, then rapidly. I stood still, my whole attention fixed upon the motions of her fingers. Suddenly I felt a misty consciousness as of something forgotten—a thrill of returning thought; and somehow the mystery of language was revealed to me. I knew then that "w-a-t-e-r" meant the wonderful cool something that was flowing over my hand. That living word awakened my soul, gave it light, hope, joy, set it free! There were barriers still, it is true, but barriers that could in time be swept away.[3]

Certainly, this was how the blind man must have felt when he saw water for the first time as he washed his eyes in the pool of Siloam.

Just as the Light of the World gave sight to the blind beggar, and just as that "living word" awakened the soul of Helen Keller, so Jesus can awaken your life with the tender touch of His hand. He can give you light, hope, joy, and freedom like you've never known before. Surely there will still be barriers in your life—but barriers that can be swept away in time.

---

3. Keller, *The Story of My Life*, p. 36.

II. Questions and Answers

What happens when the Light of the World meets a dimly burning wick of humanity? Does He rebuke it for its faint flicker? Does He snuff it out? No. Jesus tenderly takes the charred wick in His hand and kindles its flame. But the physical light Jesus brings to this man is only a glimmer of the spiritual light that will soon follow.

A. **Between neighbors and beggar.** Like reporters at a presidential press conference, the neighbors ply the beggar with questions (vv. 8–11). His answer is unadorned and unembellished, dressed only in the truth.

> And they said to him, "Where is He?" He said, "I do not know." (v. 12)

B. **Between Pharisees and beggar.** The following passage perfectly illustrates how "the light shines in the darkness; and the darkness did not comprehend it" (1:5).

> They brought to the Pharisees him who was formerly blind. Now it was a Sabbath on the day when Jesus made the clay, and opened his eyes. Again, therefore, the Pharisees also were asking him how he received his sight. And he said to them, "He applied clay to my eyes, and I washed, and I see." Therefore some of the Pharisees were saying, "This man is not from God, because He does not keep the Sabbath." (vv. 13–16a)

Juxtaposed to the newfound physical sight of the beggar is the utter spiritual blindness of the religious aristocracy. Instead of sharing the joy of a person made whole, the Pharisees grind their teeth because the miracle took place on the Sabbath.[4] But the debate soon shifts the focus from the issue of the Sabbath to the identity of this enigmatic miracle worker.

> But others were saying, "How can a man who is a sinner perform such signs?" And there was a division among them. They said therefore to the blind man again, "What do you say about Him, since He

---

4. By this time, years of legalistic accretion had encrusted the original Sabbath laws like barnacles. If a lamp ran out of oil, for example, you couldn't fill it on the Sabbath. If sandals were shod with nails, you couldn't walk in them. You couldn't trim your beard or hair or even a fingernail. And benevolent acts like setting a broken bone had to be postponed till after the Sabbath. For Jesus to make clay and then heal a person constituted unlawful work in the Pharisees' eyes. See William Barclay, *The Gospel of John,* rev. ed., The Daily Study Bible Series (Philadelphia, Pa.: Westminster Press, 1975), vol. 2, pp. 44–45. Jesus, however, indicated that the intent of the Sabbath regulations had been turned around 180 degrees from what God wanted when He declared that "the Sabbath was made for man, and not man for the Sabbath" (Mark 2:27). For other verbal altercations Jesus had with the Pharisees over this issue, see Matthew 12:1–14 and Luke 13:10–17; 14:1–6.

opened your eyes?" And he said, "He is a prophet."
(vv. 16b–17)

The Jews, however, blind to the miracle (v. 18), interrogate the beggar's parents (vv. 19–21). Intimidated by this cross-examination and afraid of being excommunicated, the parents plead ignorance (vv. 21–23). So the Pharisees return the beggar to the witness stand.

> So a second time they called the man who had been blind, and said to him, "Give glory to God; we know that this man is a sinner." He therefore answered, "Whether He is a sinner, I do not know; one thing I do know, that, whereas I was blind, now I see." (vv. 24–25)

The Mute Eloquence of a Changed Life

No testimony is quite as compelling as that of a changed life. People can argue theology and dispute interpretations of the Bible, but they are rendered speechless when confronted with the reality of a changed life. It is the unarguable apologetic. Cardinal Suhard gives us a convicting definition of such a life:

> To be a witness does not consist in engaging
> in propaganda, nor even in stirring people up,
> but in being a living mystery. It means to live
> in such a way that one's life would not make
> sense if God did not exist.[5]

Certainly this could be said of the blind man's life after he met Jesus . . . and of so many people whom Jesus touched. Can it be said of you? Is your life a cold monument to religious duty—or is it "a living mystery"?

The Pharisees continue their attack not only by denigrating Jesus (v. 24) but also by sarcastically discrediting the man Jesus has healed: "You were born entirely in sins, and are you teaching us?" (v. 34). This severe rebuke is prompted by the man's insightful comments in verses 30–33.

> The man answered and said to them, "Well, here is an amazing thing, that you do not know where He is from, and yet He opened my eyes. We know that God does not hear sinners; but if anyone is God-fearing,

---

5. As quoted by Madeleine L'Engle, *Walking on Water: Reflections on Faith and Art* (Wheaton, Ill.: Harold Shaw Publishers, 1980), p. 31.

and does His will, He hears him. Since the beginning of time it has never been heard that anyone opened the eyes of a person born blind. If this man were not from God, He could do nothing."

But in their blind pride, the Pharisees threw the formerly blind man out of the temple (v. 35a).

III. Belief and Unbelief

As Chrysostom observed, "The Jews cast him out of the Temple; the Lord of the Temple found him."[6] For the first time, the man born blind beholds the Light of the World face-to-face.

> Jesus heard that they had put him out; and finding him, He said, "Do you believe in the Son of Man?" He answered and said, "And who is He, Lord, that I may believe in Him?" Jesus said to him, "You have both seen Him, and He is the one who is talking with you." And he said, "Lord, I believe." And he worshiped Him. And Jesus said, "For judgment I came into this world, that those who do not see may see; and that those who see may become blind." Those of the Pharisees who were with Him heard these things, and said to Him, "We are not blind too, are we?" Jesus said to them, "If you were blind, you would have no sin; but since you say, 'We see,' your sin remains." (vv. 35–41)

"John evidently wants us to see that the activity of Jesus as the Light of the world inevitably results in judgment on those whose natural habitat is darkness. They oppose the Light and they bring down condemnation on themselves accordingly."[7] The other side to that coin is the restoration of sight to those who admit to their darkened condition and come out, as the blind man did, to embrace the light.

┌ A Concluding Application ─────────────────

Helen Keller nostalgically recalls her feelings about that life-changing day when she first met Anne Sullivan.

> I learned a great many new words that day. I do not remember what they all were; but I do know that *mother, father, sister, teacher* were among them —words that were to make the world blossom for me, "like Aaron's rod, with flowers." It would have

---

6. Chrysostom, as quoted by Barclay, *The Gospel of John*, vol. 2, p. 49.

7. Leon Morris, *The Gospel according to John*, rev. ed., The New International Commentary on the New Testament Series (Grand Rapids, Mich.: William B. Eerdmans Publishing Co., 1995), p. 429.

been difficult to find a happier child than I was as I lay in my crib at the close of that eventful day and lived over the joys it had brought me, and for the first time longed for a new day to come.[8]

Jesus can do that for your life. He'll make it blossom. Give you joy. Give you a reason to live—a longing for a new day to come. The Word that became flesh can incarnate Himself in your life and fill every dark corner with light.

Living Insights

Have you examined your spiritual eyesight lately? There aren't any charts on the wall to test this by, just some attitudes in your heart. Have a seat, then, and let the Holy Spirit show you any symptoms of spiritual blindness that may be dimming your ability to see and follow the Light of the World.

Do you generally feel more comfortable going by the book, keeping the rules? Where do you gain a sense of security—in doing things right or in relying on God's love? Do you expect God to play by the rules in your life? What happens when the unexpected comes? How do you handle it?

_____

_____

_____

_____

_____

_____

_____

When other Christians try to talk to you about God from a different angle than what you're used to, how do you respond to them? Are you open to learning? Do you feel threatened? Are you excited to discover something new? Do you respond angrily, rejecting both the person and their message? Is it extremely

8. Keller, *The Story of My Life*, p. 37.

important for you to be right at all times? Are you willing to prayerfully reconsider your position?

_____

_____

_____

_____

_____

_____

_____

What characterizes your heart most of the time: gratitude for God's unmerited grace toward you or satisfaction in doing what you think God wants from you? Do you find it difficult to admit need? Or are you comfortable in confessing that you don't have it all together? Do you think that maturing in Christ means that you become more spiritually self-sufficient? Why or why not?

_____

_____

_____

_____

_____

_____

_____

What is one key quality that Jesus had but the Pharisees didn't regarding the man born blind?

_____

How present is the compassion of Christ in your life? What else gives evidence of Christ's light? What shows you that you're living in His light?

_____

_____

_____

_____

_____

_____

_____

_____

If you've found some spiritual blind spots in your life—that's good! Because only by honestly facing them and bringing them to Jesus can you hope to have your vision corrected. Pretending that we're "just fine, thank you" keeps us begging in the dark—and we don't even know it. Instead, let's allow the Light of the World to lead us out of darkness and into the light of life (John 8:12). Then we can say in grateful worship, "One thing I do know. I was blind but now I see!" (9:25 NIV).

Chapter 7
The Living Door
John 10

Is there anything as horrifying as a safe place corrupted into a place of danger by those we should be able to trust?

Herve Bertrand was vulnerable from the start. Born out of wedlock, he grew up in a Catholic orphanage in Quebec. Children have so little say in their own lives, but for orphans it's even worse. They have no parent to care for what's best for them, to provide for them, to protect them. And that's what Herve needed, protection, especially on that dreadful day when the orphanage was turned into a psychiatric hospital.

> "On March 18, 1954, the nuns came in and said, 'From today, you are all crazy.' Everyone started to cry, even the nuns. Then everything changed: Our lessons stopped, and work—they called it therapy—began. I saw the bars go on the windows, the fences go up around the compound. I saw the autobuses pull up full of psychiatric patients—our new roommates. It was like a prison. And that's where I spent a quarter of my life."[1]

Quebec's premier at the time, Maurice Duplessis, made it more lucrative for institutions to care for the mentally ill than for orphans—granting three times as much money or more for their care. So orphanages were converted into psychiatric hospitals, sometimes overnight, and more than three thousand children were housed next to the mentally disturbed. These children were then treated as if they, too, were disturbed—complete with straitjackets, drugs, and dark cells. Even their medical records were changed so they would qualify for the extra monies, branding normal, healthy children as unstable or mentally retarded.

Dr. Jean Gaudreau, one of the doctors who in 1960 investigated these institutions, said of the imprisoned children, "Most of them were not retarded when they went in. Some of them were by the time they got out."[2]

Herve was sexually abused by a guard to the point that reparative surgery was recommended. "I told the nuns," he says, "but they didn't believe me."[3]

---

1. As quoted by Maggie Farley, "Mental Illness by Mandate," *Los Angeles Times,* February 10, 2000, section A.
2. As quoted by Farley, "Mental Illness by Mandate."
3. As quoted by Farley, "Mental Illness by Mandate."

How has the church in Quebec, whose job it was to nurture and help these helpless children, responded to those it harmed? Cardinal Jean-Claude Turcotte, a senior representative of the Catholic Church in Canada, dismissed the orphans as "victims of life" and coldly stated, "They don't deserve an apology." He then dodged any responsibility by blaming the children's parents for their sinful lifestyles in the first place.[4]

It's tragic when trust is betrayed, but it's especially abominable when those who claim to represent God mangle His purposes and His people. And it's not a matter of being Catholic or Protestant—corruption of God's plan, sadly, happens in all denominations in all countries in all times. It happens when religion replaces a relationship with God, when pride replaces gratitude for God's grace, when a hunger for power replaces a desire to serve.

The Pharisees, who were supposed to be the shepherds of God's people, instead ruled Israel with an iron fist. They defrauded the people with crooked practices at the temple, burdened them with rules and regulations that were never in God's Law, and clung to their power through intimidation. As we saw in our last chapter, rather than rejoicing at an obvious work of God, they excommunicated the newly healed blind man—attempting to slam the door of God in his face.

Little did they realize that they'd actually freed him from their man-made house of hell to find the true Door who opens heaven to us all. In Jesus, he found the true Shepherd of his soul, the One who heals His sheep and judges those who do them harm.

I. Historical Background

To better understand what Jesus wants to teach us about Himself, it will be helpful to familiarize ourselves with how shepherds in Israel cared for their sheep.

> Sheep were commonly herded in a walled enclosure, mostly open to the sky, but providing protection from the worst of the elements and from beasts of prey. . . . What is apparently in mind [in John 10] is a large fold where several flocks find shelter. One doorkeeper can thus look after a large number of sheep. . . . When the shepherd comes in he calls the sheep, who know his voice. The Eastern shepherd often has an individual call for each of his sheep. . . . The sheep know their shepherd and recognize the call he gives his own. More, they respond to it, and in this way he leads them out.

4. As quoted and summarized by Farley, "Mental Illness by Mandate."

When he has put all his own sheep out of the fold the shepherd leads them to their destination by walking before them. This is a very different picture from that of driving the sheep (which is more familiar in lands like Australia today).[5]

II. The Teaching of Jesus

With this understanding, Jesus' words take on greater clarity and color.

A. The instruction. The first image He uses for Himself is the door to the sheepfold.

> "Truly, truly, I say to you, he who does not enter by the door into the fold of the sheep, but climbs up some other way, he is a thief and a robber. But he who enters by the door is a shepherd of the sheep. To him the doorkeeper opens, and the sheep hear his voice, and he calls his own sheep by name, and leads them out. When he puts forth all his own, he goes before them, and the sheep follow him because they know his voice. And a stranger they simply will not follow, but will flee from him, because they do not know the voice of strangers." (John 10:1–5)

B. The interpretation. Jesus' listeners are confused by His allegory (v. 6), so He patiently explains it to them.

> "Truly, truly, I say to you, I am the door of the sheep. All who came before Me are thieves and robbers, but the sheep did not hear them. I am the door; if anyone enters through Me, he shall be saved, and shall go in and out, and find pasture." (vv. 7–10)

Jesus, as the Door, is the only way to enter eternal life. The thieves and robbers were probably both false messiahs and "the religious leaders who are more interested in fleecing the sheep than in guiding, nurturing and guarding them. They are the leaders of [chapter] 9, who should have had ears to hear Jesus' claims and recognize him as the revelation from God, but who instead belittle and expel the sheep."[6] In contrast, Jesus offers His sheep who hear His voice security and nourishment. And rather than abusing the sheep for His own

---

5. Leon Morris, *The Gospel according to John,* rev. ed., The New International Commentary on the New Testament Series (Grand Rapids, Mich.: William B. Eerdmans Publishing Co., 1995), pp. 446–47.

6. D. A. Carson, *The Gospel according to John* (Grand Rapids, Mich.: William B. Eerdmans Publishing Co., 1991), p. 382.

personal gain, as the Pharisees did, He is willing to sacrifice Himself for their good.

> "I am the good shepherd; the good shepherd lays down His life for the sheep. He who is a hireling, and not a shepherd, who is not the owner of the sheep, beholds the wolf coming, and leaves the sheep, and flees, and the wolf snatches them, and scatters them. He flees because he is a hireling, and is not concerned about the sheep. I am the good shepherd; and I know My own, and My own know Me, even as the Father knows Me and I know the Father; and I lay down My life for the sheep." (vv. 11–15)

As the Good Shepherd, Jesus doesn't run to save Himself when there is danger; He puts Himself between the danger and His sheep. He and His own know and love one another intimately, just as Jesus and His Father do. What a beautiful picture of Jesus' loving care!

C. **The revelation.** Jesus next asserts that His care extends beyond the fold of Israel.

> "And I have other sheep, which are not of this fold; I must bring them also, and they shall hear My voice; and they shall become one flock with one shepherd. For this reason the Father loves Me, because I lay down My life that I may take it again. No one has taken it away from Me, but I lay it down on My own initiative. I have authority to lay it down, and I have authority to take it up again. This commandment I received from My Father." (vv. 16–18)

These two distinct groups of sheep symbolize two separate bodies of believers. The "fold" is clearly a reference to those of Jewish ancestry who had accepted Jesus as their Messiah. The "other sheep," then, would be the Gentile believers. The two groups would become one fold, but only through the sacrificial death of the Shepherd (compare Gal. 3:28; Eph. 2, especially vv. 13, 15–16).

The Story of the Good Shepherd

The story of the Good Shepherd is not the tragic story of a victim but the tremendous story of a victor— One who secured His victory by voluntarily laying His life down on our behalf.

Pilate tried to intimidate Jesus with the authority to release Him or crucify Him (John 19:10). Peter tried to protect Him with his sword at Gethsemane (Matt. 26:51;

John 18:10). But Jesus' death was voluntary. He told Peter, "Put your sword back into its place. . . . . Or do you think that I cannot appeal to My Father, and He will at once put at My disposal more than twelve legions of angels?" (Matt. 26:52–53). And to Pilate, Jesus replied, "You would have no authority over Me, unless it had been given you from above" (John 19:11).

No, Jesus did not become entrapped in some sticky political web from which He could not extricate Himself. Rather, He spun a story of selfless sacrifice so enticing, so enchanting, that it would attract people to Him for millennia to come.

And we, those "other sheep," have come into the fold because that two-thousand-year-old story stirred us like nothing else—that story of a Shepherd so supremely good that nothing stood in the way of His love for His sheep.

Not even His own life.

III. The Reaction of the Jews

The Jews' reactions are mixed (v. 19): some hate Jesus, castigating Him as satanic or psychotic (v. 20); others, though as yet uncommitted, are convinced His words and deeds could not be attributed to demonic power (v. 21). The dissension remains unresolved as the curtain abruptly falls on this scene.

IV. The Hostile Discussion

The curtain reopens to a winter set during the Feast of the Dedication in Jerusalem.

A. The setting. The scene is Solomon's porch (vv. 22–23), elegantly roofed and colonnaded with magnificent forty-foot stone pillars. Here rabbis walk with their students, discussing and debating the hot theological issues of the day.

B. The dialogue. Jesus picks up where He left off—in a discussion revolving around the question of His identity. Jesus appeals to His works and His words, claiming that only the Messiah could perform the deeds He has done.

The Jews therefore gathered around Him, and were saying to Him, "How long will You keep us in suspense? If You are the Christ, tell us plainly." Jesus answered them, "I told you, and you do not believe; the works that I do in My Father's name, these bear witness of Me. But you do not believe, because you are not of My sheep. My sheep hear My voice, and I know them, and they follow Me; and I give eternal life to them, and they shall never perish; and no one shall snatch them out of My hand. My Father, who has given them to Me, is greater than all; and no one is able to snatch them out of the Father's hand. I and the Father are one." (vv. 24–30) Jesus' return to sheep imagery in verses 26–29 provides us with four qualities of genuine believers: they are sensitive to His voice, obedient to His leadership, confident of their destiny, and secure in the Shepherd's strong and loving arms.

C. **The rejection.** But the response of these Jews indicates that they are recalcitrant goats rather than obedient sheep. For instead of running to the Shepherd, they prefer to butt heads with Him (vv. 31–39). The question of Jesus' identity is unambiguously settled, but they will not accept it. With stones in hand, this Jewish jury declares His sentence: "For a good work we do not stone You, but for blasphemy; and because You, being a man, make Yourself out to be God" (v. 33).

Genuine Reception

John tells us earlier in his Gospel that Jesus "came to His own, and those who were His own did not receive Him" (1:11). He came to shepherd a wayward bunch of rebel goats, but they lowered their stubborn heads and pawed the ground in opposition to Him.

Now, most probably, you are not a goat but a sheep. But what kind of sheep are you?

Are you sensitive to His voice when He speaks to you in His Word? How about when He speaks to you through your conscience? Or through other people? God spoke to Balaam through a donkey. Certainly, He could speak to you through an obstinate acquaintance . . . or through a strong-willed child . . . or through some circumstance that has plopped itself smack-dab in front of you, staring you stubbornly in the face.

Are you obedient to His voice? It's one thing to hear; it's quite another to act on what you've heard. His sheep are to be not only hearers but doers of His word as well (James 1:22–25).

Are you confident in your destiny? Are you secure in your relationship with Christ? Remember, you're in the Good Shepherd's invincible hands—hands that even Satan himself cannot pry open!

The shepherd imagery that Jesus used would not have been anything new to His listeners. The Old Testament is rich with pictures of God tenderly shepherding His people—and rightly judging those who failed to shepherd His people as they were supposed to. Let's take some time to get acquainted with these pictures that surely would have been in Jesus' mind as He was describing Himself. Jot down what they teach you about false shepherds, what characterizes the Good Shepherd, and what is dear to God's heart.

Psalm 23 _____

_____

_____

_____

_____

_____

Isaiah 40:11 _____

_____

_____

Jeremiah 23:1–4 _____

_____

_____

_____

_____

Jeremiah 50:6–7 _____

_____

_____

_____

Ezekiel 34 _____

_____

_____

_____

_____

_____

_____

Micah 5:4–5a _____

_____

_____

If you are a shepherd of God's people, how does your leadership stack up in light of the characteristics communicated in these passages? How about in the light of Christ's self-sacrificing model?

_____

_____

_____

_____

_____

_____

What, if anything, would you like to change?

_____

_____

_____

_____

Dedicate this matter to prayer, won't you? Jesus gladly helps those who bring their needs to Him, and He wants to give you and those He's given you to shepherd fullness of life (John 10:10)!

Chapter 8

Back from Beyond

John 11

Death is usually the last thing we want to talk about. It makes us feel uncomfortable, awkward, and we recoil when someone brings the subject up. One of the reasons we fear death is that, in spite of all our medical achievements, we haven't been able to conquer it.

> The hearse began its grievous journey many thousand years ago, as a litter made of saplings.
>
> Litter, sled, wagon, Cadillac: the conveyance has changed, but the corpse it carries is the same. Birth and death enclose man in a sort of parenthesis of the present. And the brackets at the beginning and end of life are still impenetrable.
>
> This frustrates us, especially in a time of scientific break-through and exploding knowledge, that we should be able to break out of earth's environment and yet be stopped cold by death's unyielding mystery. Electroencephalogram may replace mirror held before the mouth, autopsies may become more sophisticated, cosmetic embalming may take the place of pennies on the eyelids and canvas shrouds, but death continues to confront us with its blank wall. Everything changes; death is changeless.
>
> We may postpone it, we may tame its violence, but death is still there waiting for us.
>
> Death always waits. The door of the hearse is never closed.[1]

In this chapter, we are going to penetrate, however slightly, that unyielding mystery. We're going to examine the account of a man raised from the dead—a man brought back from beyond—by the only One who has conquered death, Jesus Christ.

I. Theological Backdrop

Before we enter into the rich emotions of this story, let's gain an understanding of how this incident fits into the greater scheme of John's Gospel. The raising of Lazarus from the dead is the seventh and last sign of Jesus that John records. It is the climactic sign because it illustrates beyond doubt Jesus' power to give life (5:21) and triumph over death. All that Jesus has done and said before—

---

1. Joseph Bayly, *The Last Thing We Talk About,* rev. ed. (Elgin, Ill.: David C. Cook Publishing Co., 1973), p. 11.

- His claim that only through believing in Him can we have eternal life (John 3:15–16),

- His offer of the water of life (4:14; 7:37–38),

- His saving the life of the royal official's son (vv. 46–54),

- His offering Himself as the Bread of Life (6:33, 35, 40, 47–48, 53–58),

- His being the Light of the World who grants us the light of life (8:12),

- His opening the way to abundant, eternal life as the living Door (10:7–10)

—all these are crystallized and affirmed in His living proof that He is the Resurrection and the Life (11:25–26). Even more than that, this sign prefigures Jesus' own approaching death and resurrection —His laying down His life for His sheep and then taking it up again as the Good Shepherd (10:11–18)—as Lesslie Newbigin explains.

> This miracle most fitly concludes the series of signs and forms the transition to the story of the passion . . . [because] it shows that Jesus gives life only by giving his life. The raising of Lazarus leads directly to the death of Jesus [11:45–53]. It is at the cost of life that he gives life. The "abundant life" that he gives is life through death. He is the life only because he is the resurrection from the dead (v. 25). It is in this sense that the illness of Lazarus is for the glory of God (v. 4).[2]

With this foundation laid, let's now watch and learn from Jesus as He tenderly ministers to His grieving friends.

II. The Sickness of Lazarus

About two miles outside of Jerusalem lay the sleepy hamlet of Bethany, a parenthesis of peace where Jesus often found rest and relaxation in the home of Lazarus and his two sisters, Martha and Mary. But all is not peaceful this particular day—Lazarus is deathly ill (John 11:1–2). In desperation, the sisters send for Jesus.

"Lord, behold, he whom You love is sick." (v. 3)

III. The Response of Jesus

Verse 5 reveals that "Jesus loved Martha, and her sister, and Lazarus." In light of that, you would expect Jesus to drop everything and come running to Lazarus' bedside. But curiously, Jesus delays

2. Lesslie Newbigin, *The Light Has Come: An Exposition of the Fourth Gospel* (Grand Rapids, Mich.: William B. Eerdmans Publishing Co., 1982), p. 138.

for two days (v. 6). Was He too busy? Was He attending to other matters of greater importance? No. The purpose for the delay was twofold: one, "for the glory of God, that the Son of God may be glorified by it" (v. 4); and two, "so that you may believe" (v. 15).

Coping with Crisis

In times of crisis, it is essential that we understand some important facts about *time* and *perspective*.

Regarding time, our Lord is never late. He often delays His response, but He is never late. His watch is merely set to a different timetable, calibrated to matters of eternal rather than temporal consequence.

Regarding perspective, we can adopt either a human or a divine outlook. The human perspective focuses on the urgent and blurs the important. It concentrates on our immediate rather than our ultimate welfare, on our temporary good instead of God's eternal glory. The divine perspective, however, factors eternity into the enigmatic equations of life. While the human perspective pleads, "*My* will be done, *now*," the divine perspective makes its request, yet patiently adds, "Nevertheless, not my will be done, but Thine."

How is your vision and sense of divine timing during trials? Do you see only the crisis—or do you see Christ's hand behind, before, below, above, and within that crisis? And have you checked your spiritual watch lately? Is it synchronized with eternity? Is it keeping His time—or your own?

IV. The Reactions of Mary and Martha

By the time Jesus finally comes to Bethany, Lazarus has died and has been in the tomb for four days (v. 17). Christ's arrival sparks reactions in Mary and Martha—reactions that are both similar and dissimilar. Note the contrast in verse 20:

Martha therefore, when she heard that Jesus was coming, went to meet Him; but Mary still sat in the house.

But notice the similarity of their initial greetings. First Martha's:

"Lord, if You had been here, my brother would not have died." (v. 21)

Then Mary's:

Therefore, when Mary came where Jesus was, she saw Him, and fell at His feet, saying to Him, "Lord, if You had been here, my brother would not have died." (v. 32)

Although their words are the same, their posture is not. Martha runs to Him, active and erect; Mary falls at His feet, passive and prostrate. Hurting and confused, but still believing in Jesus, Martha brings the questions of her heart to her Friend.

> "Even now I know that whatever You ask of God, God will give You." Jesus said to her, "Your brother shall rise again." Martha said to Him, "I know that he will rise again in the resurrection on the last day." Jesus said to her, "I am the resurrection and the life; he who believes in Me shall live even if he dies, and everyone who lives and believes in Me shall never die. Do you believe this?" (vv. 22–26)

With this question reaching out to her, Martha grasps the truth with open arms, even though she doesn't yet fully understand what Jesus means (see vv. 39–40).

> She said to Him, "Yes, Lord; I have believed that You are the Christ, the Son of God, even He who comes into the world." (v. 27)

Martha needed intellectual buttressing, but Mary needs emotional support.

> When Jesus therefore saw [Mary] weeping, and the Jews who came with her, also weeping, He was deeply moved in spirit, and was troubled, and said, "Where have you laid him?" They said to Him, "Lord, come and see." Jesus wept. And so the Jews were saying, "Behold how He loved him!" (vv. 33–36)

Martha needed to know that Jesus was in control. Mary needed to know that Jesus cared. And without rebukes or reservations, He met each sister where she was, whether standing or prostrate and whether needing intellectual or emotional support.

⌐ If Only ─────────────────

Those two regretful words. How broad the blame that's placed on their narrow shoulders!

"If only we hadn't moved here . . ."

"If only I hadn't married him . . ."

"If only I hadn't listened to her . . ."

"If only we had more money . . ."

What are your "if onlys"? Won't you take them to Jesus, like Mary and Martha did? Let Him assure you, as He did those forlorn sisters, that He is in control—and that He cares.

V. The Raising of Lazarus

Jesus then comes to the tomb, that stone testimony of a creation gone tragically awry. And again He grieves (v. 38). Tersely, with restrained anger at the briery wilderness Satan has made of His

Edenic creation, Jesus instructs the onlookers: "Remove the stone" (v. 39a). Once the stone is removed, Jesus prays that those watching would know God sent Him (vv. 41–42), then shouts: "Lazarus, come forth" (v. 43). And, like an eerie scene from *The Mummy's Tomb,* Lazarus comes forth—back from beyond (v. 44). Don't you wonder what stories he could tell? What must it have felt like to hear the voice of his Friend, the Lord and Giver of life, call his name and free him from the grave? From this dramatic event that quaked the Judean countryside, two tremors of truth ripple through the centuries to touch our lives today:

- When delay occurs, God has a better time and a better way.

- When death occurs, God has a better plan and a better purpose.

Happily, many of the Jews believed in Jesus as a result of this miracle (v. 45). But not everyone entered into the joy of life. It's almost beyond belief, but the Pharisees, when told of what Jesus did (v. 46), "turn[ed] from the light of life to the darkness of death."[3]

VI. The Plotting of the Religious Leaders

Where Jesus seeks God's glory, the religious leaders scheme to hold onto their earthly power and prestige.

> Therefore the chief priests and the Pharisees convened a council, and were saying, "What are we doing? For this man is performing many signs. If we let Him go on like this, all men will believe in Him, and the Romans will come and take away both *our* place and *our* nation." (vv. 47–48, emphasis added)

This council of the chief priests and Pharisees was known as the Sanhedrin, who, under Rome's watchful eye, had the political and religious authority in Israel. As Jesus' popularity grew, the Sanhedrin worried that so would the people's desire for a messiah who would overthrow Rome's rule. Rome, of course, would quash this rebellion and set up their own rule, ousting the existing leaders. The bottom line? The religious leaders cared more about their political status and power on earth than they did about whether Jesus really was sent from God. As Bruce Milne notes,

> The guardians of the sacred traditions of Israel were reduced to the level of political functionaries. . . . Right has become equated with the avoidance of trouble and the preservation of their hold on power. Thus the cause of the living God, the glory of the age-old revelation from the patriarchs through the Red Sea and Mount Sinai, is

3. Newbigin, *The Light Has Come,* p. 145.

all mortgaged in one sorry impassioned hour to save their political skins.[4]

Rebuking his fearful colleagues, the high priest, Caiaphas, proposes a simple, lethal solution.

> But a certain one of them, Caiaphas, who was high priest that year, said to them, "You know nothing at all, nor do you take into account that it is expedient for you that one man should die for the people, and that the whole nation should not perish." Now this he did not say on his own initiative; but being high priest that year, he prophesied that Jesus was going to die for the nation, and not for the nation only, but that He might also gather together into one the children of God who are scattered abroad. So from that day on they planned together to kill Him. (vv. 49–53)

For giving life, these men will put Jesus to death. Little do they realize, though, that they will be fulfilling God's own plan to sacrifice His Son on our behalf. The timing, however, is still in Jesus' hands, so He leaves that area for a remote city near the wilderness, where He and His disciples await the right time (v. 54). As Passover nears, the "Lamb of God who takes away the sin of the world" (1:29) begins to make His final preparations before He lays down His life and takes it up again (vv. 55–57)—coming back from beyond with life in His hands for all who will believe in Him!

Living Insights

Many of us Christians often feel that bringing glory to God means putting on a happy face no matter what is happening in our lives. If we're sad, angry, confused, or hurting, we somehow feel that if we don't have these difficult feelings wrapped up neatly in a moment's time, we've betrayed the faith and put a blot on our testimony to Jesus.

Does Jesus feel this way about us and our feelings? Reread John 11:1–44. How did Jesus deal with His disciples' worries (vv. 1–16)?

_____

_____

_____

4. Milne, *The Message of John: Here Is Your King!*, The Bible Speaks Today Series (Downers Grove, Ill.: InterVarsity Press, 1993), p. 173.

How did He handle Martha's grief (vv. 17–27)?

_____

_____

_____

_____

What was His response to Mary's broken heart (vv. 28–33)?

_____

_____

_____

_____

What was Jesus' own response to the death of Lazarus (vv. 34–38)?

_____

_____

_____

_____

Did He once say to anyone, "Stop crying!" or, "How dare you ask Me a question!" No, He is gentle with His people, knowing that our sin-marred world often breaks our hearts.

When you grieve, when you're confused, yes, and even when you're angry, don't try to hide your feelings from God and pretend everything's alright. He knows you better than that. And since He is the Truth, He can handle the truth. Remember,

> We have a great high priest who has passed through the heavens, Jesus the Son of God. . . . We do not have a high priest who cannot sympathize with our weaknesses, but one who has been tempted in all things as we are, yet without sin. Let us therefore draw near with confidence to the throne of grace, that we may receive mercy and may find grace to help in time of need. (Heb. 4:14–16)

Chapter 9

Seeking before Hiding

John 12

From his days on the pediatric staff of USC Medical Center in Los Angeles, Dr. James Dobson tells the story of a five-year-old boy dying of lung cancer. Many parents of terminally ill children can't handle the pressure and grief and, consequently, let the children die alone. But this little boy's mother came to his hospital room every day, holding him, rocking him, loving him.

One night, after the mother had gone home, the nurses heard the child talking in his room, saying over and over, "I hear the bells! I hear the bells! They're ringing!" They assumed he was hallucinating and told his mother so the next morning.

"He was not hallucinating," she replied. "Weeks ago, I told my boy that when the pain got so bad that he couldn't breathe, he'd soon be going to heaven to be with Jesus. And when that pain got too bad, he was to look up toward heaven and listen for the bells. They'd be ringing. They'd be ringing for him."

With that, she turned into his room, gathered her son in her arms, and rocked him into the waiting arms of God.

What a picture of peace. That mother and son could face death because they had security in Jesus Christ. They had accepted His plan.

In John 12, Jesus begins his last week on earth. Pain, rejection, and death await Him, yet He can face it all because He has accepted God's plan, "entrusting Himself to Him who judges righteously" (1 Pet. 2:23).

I. A Survey of the Final Week

After Jesus brought Lazarus back to life, the infuriated Pharisees made serious plans to kill Him. Jesus would make His sacrifice in His own time, however, so He withdrew with His disciples to Ephraim, a remote city north of Jerusalem, on the edge of the Judean desert (John 11:53–54). At this juncture, Jesus begins to alter His ministry. First, He changes His public outreach to a private one—He moves from seeking the multitudes to sequestering Himself with the disciples (see 12:36b). Second, He shifts His emphasis away from signs and concentrates on quiet, intimate conversation with His disciples (chaps. 13–17). In fact, the raising of Lazarus is the last sign until His own Resurrection. And third, He reduces His travels, returning to Jerusalem and staying there (12:12). He's not out evangelizing; He's preparing to leave and preparing the disciples for His departure.

What about Your Last Week?

If you knew you had only one more week to live, how would you spend your time? What's really important to you? Look closely at Christ's last days before the Cross. He chose to spend His final moments with those most dear, with His closest friends. This week, this day, could be your last. How are you investing your time?

II. A Study of the First Part of the Week

As this last week unfolds, the things Jesus does and says are of top priority. He's still in the public eye at the beginning of the week, and John captures three events in his twelfth chapter.

A. Six days before (vv. 1–11). After His sojourn in Ephraim, Jesus is back in Bethany as the guest of honor at a dinner party. Relaxing around the table with Him are the disciples and Lazarus. While Martha serves them, Mary enters the room with a dramatic gesture.

> Mary therefore took a pound of very costly perfume of pure nard, and anointed the feet of Jesus, and wiped His feet with her hair; and the house was filled with the fragrance of the perfume.[1] (v. 3)

Mary performs this worshipful act of love with no regard for appearance. Respectable Jewish women never let their hair down in public, nor did they sit around the dinner table with Jewish men. But Judas, in faulting her behavior, doesn't condemn her for those things; he condemns her extravagance.

> "Why was this perfume not sold for three hundred denarii, and given to poor people?" (v. 5)

That sounds noble, doesn't it? But in the sixty years between Judas' act and the time this book was written, John has learned that Judas' response was not so pure.

> Now he said this, not because he was concerned about the poor, but because he was a thief, and as he had the money box, he used to pilfer what was put into it. (v. 6)

---

1. "Many scholars have seen a double meaning here. They have taken it to mean that the whole Church was filled with the sweet memory of Mary's action. A lovely deed becomes the possession of the whole world and adds to the beauty of life in general, something which time cannot ever take away." William Barclay, *The Gospel of John*, rev. ed., The Daily Study Bible Series (Philadelphia, Pa.: Westminster Press, 1975), vol. 2, p. 111.

Judas is the treasurer for the disciples, the most trusted man in the group. But Jesus, who sees fully the betrayal in his heart (see v. 4), defends Mary's selfless devotion.

> "Let her alone, in order that she may keep it for the day of My burial. For the poor you always have with you, but you do not always have Me." (vv. 7–8)

Mary is preparing Jesus' body for burial, while Judas will prepare His death (see 13:2).

The Other Guest

John says that this dinner party is for Jesus (v. 2), but another guest draws quite a bit of attention too. In verse 9, we see that a great multitude has gathered outside the house, not just to see Jesus, "but that they might also see Lazarus, whom He raised from the dead."

Lazarus is a living miracle, and, by merely living, he's spreading the gospel. No wonder the chief priests want Lazarus dead too (v. 10)—his very life proves Jesus' claims.[2]

Like Lazarus, our lives speak the gospel to others. For good or for bad, we influence those around us every day. Are we drawing them to Christ? Or are we pushing them away?

B. Five days before (vv. 12–19). John next transports us from the sleepy village of Bethany to the bustling metropolis of Jerusalem. With Passover just five days away, the city is bursting with people who have come to celebrate. Most of them had either witnessed Jesus bringing Lazarus out of the tomb or had at least heard about it. Now this miracle worker is coming to their city!

> When they heard that Jesus was coming to Jerusalem, [they] took the branches of the palm trees, and went out to meet Him, and began to cry out, "Hosanna![3] Blessed is He who comes in the name of the Lord, even the King of Israel." And Jesus, finding a young donkey, sat on it; as it is written, "Fear not, daughter of Zion; behold, your King is coming, seated on a donkey's colt." (vv. 12b–15; see also Zech. 9:9)

---

2. Virtually all the priests were Sadducees, who did not believe in the resurrection of the dead.

3. Translated from the Hebrew and Greek, *hosanna* means "save, we pray" or "save, now."

The Pharisees can't believe their eyes. More and more people, hearing about the miracle with Lazarus, kept putting their faith in this Jesus, this local man who was causing so much trouble for them (vv. 17–18).

> The Pharisees therefore said to one another, "You see that you are not doing any good; look, the world has gone after Him." (v. 19)

Blaming each other, they realize they've lost their grip on the people's hearts.

C. **Four days before** (vv. 20–50). Again John changes the scene without warning, introducing a third set of characters.

> Now there were certain Greeks among those who were going up to worship at the feast; these therefore came to Philip, who was from Bethsaida of Galilee, and began to ask him, saying, "Sir, we wish to see Jesus." (vv. 20–21)

The Greeks were God-fearing Gentiles who were probably not yet proselytes but still admired much of what they saw in Judaism and came regularly to the feasts.[4] Because Philip has a Greek name, perhaps this group thinks he will be sympathetic to their request. Unsure of what to do, Philip goes to Andrew, and together they bring the request to Jesus[5] (v. 22).

> And Jesus answered them, saying, "The hour has come for the Son of Man to be glorified." (v. 23)

Jesus responds as though the Greeks aren't even present. His mind is preoccupied with one thing—His death. From verse 23 through the end of the chapter, Jesus presents His last public teaching, concentrating on four major themes. First, the Cross is imminent, only four days away (vv. 23–28, 32). Second, the pain is great (v. 27). Third, the need is urgent (vv. 35–36). Fourth, the response will be varied—some will accept Him, while others will reject Him (vv. 37, 42, 43). Throughout this passage we see continual reminders of the closeness between Father and Son. Jesus anguishes over the Cross, and His anguish is real, but an abiding peace steadies Him through the pain. He has accepted His Father's sovereign plan, which was designed before the creation of the world.

---

4. See D. A. Carson, *The Gospel according to John* (Grand Rapids, Mich.: William B. Eerdmans Publishing Co., 1991), p. 436.

5. Andrew is mentioned three times in the Bible, and each time he is bringing someone to Christ (see John 1:40–42; 6:8–9).

"For I did not speak on My own initiative, but the Father Himself who sent Me has given Me commandment, what to say, and what to speak. And I know that His commandment is eternal life; therefore the things I speak, I speak just as the Father has told Me." (vv. 49–50)

III. A Summary of the Truth

We can glean three principles from our study of these last days in Jesus' life.

A. Salvation is not limited to certain types. Remember Judas? He was Christ's disciple, the trusted treasurer. But he defected. Mary was emotional and unconventional, yet she embraced Christ with all her heart. Likewise, the Jews in the street believed Him, the Greeks were in awe of Him, but the religious officials rejected Him.

B. Worship is not limited to specific times. We can worship God anywhere and at any time. Mary worshiped at the dinner table. The crowd worshiped in the street. The Greeks worshiped as He spoke. There is no limit to when we can worship, and sometimes our most meaningful worship times are spontaneous.

C. Christianity is not lived on selfish terms. The Christian life is a paradox: to keep, we must give . . . to be great, we must serve . . . to live, we must die. And not until we die will we realize the real joy of giving, or the emptiness of keeping.

Living Insights

As we studied John 12, we saw the beginning of Christ's last week on earth.[6] John devoted chapters 12–17 to the final preparation of Jesus' disciples, and the other Gospel writers recorded it at length in their accounts as well to underscore the importance of what Jesus said and did during this time.

To get a fuller picture of the words and events leading up to the Cross, invest some time today in reading these accounts. Read Matthew 21:1–26:35; Mark 11:1–14:31; Luke 19:11–22:38; and John 12–17. No need for charts or notes—just read and reflect.

---

6. This Living Insight has been adapted from the original study guide, *Following Christ . . . the Man of God,* coauthored by Ken Gire with Living Insights by Bill Butterworth, from the Bible-teaching ministry of Charles R. Swindoll (Fullerton, Calif.: Insight for Living, 1987), p. 62.

Final Week: From Public To Private
According to John's Gospel

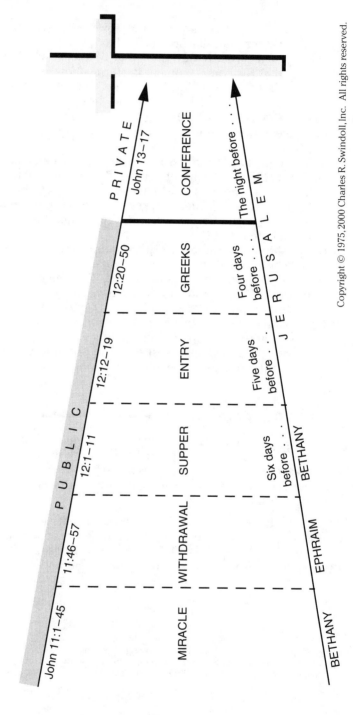

Chapter 10
Humility Personified
John 13:1–17

Humility. Confucius called it "the solid foundation of all the virtues."[1] The Greek word means "low" or "to stoop low," and it carries the idea of serving another person. That is clearly the usage in Matthew 11:28–29.

> "Come to Me, all who are weary and heavy-laden, and I will give you rest. Take My yoke upon you, and learn from Me, for I am gentle and humble in heart; and You shall find rest for your souls."

It is Christ's example of humility that Paul appeals to in his exhortation to serve one another.

> Do nothing from selfishness or empty conceit, but with humility of mind let each of you regard one another as more important than himself; do not merely look out for your own personal interests, but also for the interests of others. Have this attitude in yourselves which was also in Christ Jesus, who, although He existed in the form of God, did not regard equality with God a thing to be grasped, but emptied Himself, taking the form of a bond-servant, and being made in the likeness of men. And being found in appearance as a man, He humbled Himself by becoming obedient to the point of death, even death on a cross. (Phil. 2:3–8)

In the shadow of that cross, Jesus spent His last night and last meal with the disciples. There we see Him, not seated at the place of honor, but assuming the lowly position of a servant. And there we see Him exemplifying servanthood to the disciples—by washing their feet.

I. Background and Setting

The location for the Last Supper is Jerusalem; the occasion, the night before the Passover.

> Now before the Feast of the Passover, Jesus knowing that His hour had come that He should depart out of this world to the Father, having loved His own who were in the world, He loved them to the end. (John 13:1–2)

Just before His first miracle, Jesus told His mother that His hour had not yet come (2:4). Now that hour is fast approaching. His life

---

1. As quoted in *Five Thousand Quotations for All Occasions*, ed. Lewis C. Henry (Garden City, N.Y.: Doubleday and Co., 1945), p. 126.

and ministry are winding down to an eleventh-hour climax, and all heaven will stop for the tolling of that mournful bell. This hour doesn't creep up on Christ and overtake Him unaware, yet His eyes never stray to the clock to watch the seconds of His life tick away. Our passage indicates that He knows His time has come (13:1). He knows He has less than fifteen hours to live. But His brow is not knit in anxiety. His eyes do not dart nervously back and forth for a way of escape. He knows death is His destiny. He knows that not only is His death the Father's will (Isa. 53:10), but even His betrayal is too (John 13:2; compare Luke 22:22).

> Jesus [knew] that the Father had given all things into His hands, and that He had come forth from God, and was going back to God. (John 13:3)

II. Illustrating Humility

As time moves forward in dicing and deliberate steps, Christ's every word is weighed; every movement measured.

> [Jesus] rose from supper, and laid aside His garments; and taking a towel, He girded Himself about. Then He poured water into the basin, and began to wash the disciples' feet, and to wipe them with the towel with which He was girded. (vv. 4–5)

A. Reasons. There are at least two reasons why Jesus chooses this activity on His last night with His disciples.

1. Their hearts are proud. Christ gathered His friends to tell them of His impending suffering and betrayal (Luke 22:15, 21–22), but in the midst of His discussion the disciples get into a petty argument about rank . . . an ongoing dispute they have pursued all too often.

> And they began to discuss among themselves which one of them it might be who was going to do this thing.
>
> And there arose also a dispute among them as to which one of them was regarded to be greatest. (22:23–24; see also 9:46)

2. Their feet are dirty. As Jesus' troubled eyes fall on the disciples' tired and travel-worn feet, He seizes the opportunity both to end the argument and to instruct them in a lesson they will never forget. Craig S. Keener illuminates Jesus' actions with this historical background.

> After travelers had come a long distance, the host was to provide water for their feet as a sign of hospitality. . . . Yet loosing sandals and personally washing someone else's feet was considered servile, most commonly the

72

work of a servant or of very submissive wives or children.[2]

But no servants grace this somber banquet; no one in this crowd stoops to wash anyone's feet. The disciples are ready to fight for a throne but not for a towel. So Jesus assumes the role, demonstrating that He did "not come to be served, but to serve" (Matt. 20:28).

B. Principles. In verses 4–12, four principles emerge regarding humility.

1. Humility is unannounced. Jesus does not say: "OK, men, I'm now going to demonstrate humility!" On the contrary, Jesus abhors such obvious self-exaltation, as His teaching concerning the scribes and Pharisees indicates:

> "And they love the place of honor at banquets, and the chief seats in the synagogues, and respectful greetings in the market places, and being called by men, Rabbi. But do not be called Rabbi; for One is your Teacher, and you are all brothers. And do not call anyone on earth your father; for One is your Father, He who is in heaven. And do not be called leaders; for One is your Leader, that is, Christ. But the greatest among you shall be your servant. And whoever exalts himself shall be humbled; and whoever humbles himself shall be exalted." (Matt. 23:6–12)

No, greatness does not consist of exaltation but self-sacrifice (Phil. 2:8–9; 1 Pet. 5:5–6). As nature teaches us, the branch most full of fruit bends the lowest. Turning back to John 13, we'll see what at first glance appears to be humility. But we find that, in reality, it is only a thin veil concealing Peter's pride.

> Then He poured water into the basin, and began to wash the disciples' feet, and to wipe them with the towel with which He was girded. And so He came to Simon Peter. He said to Him, "Lord, do You wash my feet?" Jesus answered and said to him, "What I do you do not realize now, but you shall understand hereafter." (John 13:5–7)

---

2. Craig S. Keener, *The IVP Bible Background Commentary: New Testament* (Downers Grove, Ill.: InterVarsity Press, 1993), p. 297.

Embarrassed to admit his need, Peter is resistant and unwilling to submit.

2. **Humility is willing to receive—without embarrassment.** Tucking his feet under himself, Peter pulls away. Jesus stoops, but Peter resists . . . a resistance that leads to rebuke.

> Peter said to Him, "Never shall You wash my feet!" Jesus answered him, "If I do not wash you, you have no part with Me." (v. 8)

3. **Humility is not a sign of weakness.** Although performing a subservient task, Jesus can boldly assert: "Peter, you're in error!" In response, Peter swings to the other side of the pendulum.

> Simon Peter said to Him, "Lord, not my feet only, but also my hands and my head." (v. 9)

With discernment and strength, Jesus puts His finger on the pulse of a critical theological matter.

> "He who has bathed needs only to wash his feet, but is completely clean; and you are clean, but not all of you." (v. 10)

John helps us see the subtle yet significant distinction through the use of two different Greek terms, one meaning "bathed," the other meaning "wash" or "sponge." The idea is this: *once bathed, always bathed.* Customarily, people bathed in the privacy of their homes before attending a dinner engagement. But their feet would get dirty walking through the dusty streets to the host's home. When they arrived, what they needed was not a bath, but only a sponging off of their feet. Spiritually, God bathes us at conversion, cleansing our scarlet sins white as snow. But walking through life's dirty streets, we pick up some of the world's grunge and grime. What we need in that case is not another bath—just cleansing. As 1 John 1:9 states:

> If we confess our sins, He is faithful and righteous to forgive us our sins and to cleanse us from all unrighteousness.

Returning to John 13, we see a parenthetical clarification of Jesus' comment at the end of verse 10.

> For He knew the one who was betraying Him; for this reason He said, "Not all of you are clean." (v. 11)

4. **Humility does not play favorites.** It is neither selective nor exclusive. Jesus washes each foot—even Judas'. If Jesus were only human, He probably would have been

tempted to use boiling water to wash Peter's feet and ice-cold water to wash Judas'. But He didn't come to scold or to shun; He came to serve . . . gently and humbly.

III. Discussing Humility

When Jesus finishes, He reclines at the table (v. 12), and a hush settles over the room. All are looking down at their cleansed and refreshed feet, suddenly self-conscious and ashamed. In perfect teacherly fashion, Jesus draws them in with an approach that drives His message into their hearts.

A. The approach. With a penetrating question, Jesus makes sure His message is clearly understood.

"Do you know what I have done to you? You call Me Teacher and Lord; and you are right, for so I am. If I then, the Lord and the Teacher, washed your feet, you also ought to wash one another's feet. For I gave you an example that you also should do as I did to you. Truly, truly, I say to you, a slave is not greater than his master; neither is one who is sent greater than the one who sent him. If you know these things, you are blessed if you do them." (vv. 12b–17)

B. The application. Two lessons emerge from this example. One, humility includes serving one another, not just the Lord. Two, happiness results from demonstrating humility, not just learning about it.

--- *A Concluding Thought about Our God* ---

Who is like the Lord our God,
Who is enthroned on high,
Who humbles Himself to behold
The things that are in heaven and in the
    earth?
He raises the poor from the dust,
And lifts the needy from the ash heap,
To make them sit with princes,
With the princes of His people. (Ps. 113:5–8)

Living Insights

A humble God.

Think about that. The sovereign, all-powerful Creator and Controller of the universe . . . is humble.

He stoops to meet our needs. And not our clean-and-polite needs, but our dirty-feet needs—the dirty feet of pride, the dirty feet of insensitivity, the dirty feet of selfishness.

And this was the Father's will for Jesus! Remember what He said at the end of John 12?

> "I did not speak of my own accord, but the Father who sent me commanded me what to say and how to say it. I know that his command leads to eternal life. So whatever I say is just what the Father has told me to say." (vv. 49–50 NIV)

Rather than sending His Son to judge and destroy us in our sins, He sent Him to save and cleanse us, to lead us out of darkness and into light (v. 46). To wash our dirty feet and teach us how to live as cleansed people.

That's gentle, merciful humility.

Have you humbled yourself to receive His humble care? Or have you tucked your feet underneath you, as Peter did, too proud to let Jesus deal with your needs His way?

_____

_____

_____

_____

_____

Are you willing to follow Peter's example and change your heart? What needs must you allow Jesus to take care of?

_____

_____

_____

_____

For some of us, letting Jesus stoop to take care of us is not a struggle; we're comfortable keeping our relationship strictly between Him and ourselves. The hard part comes when we're challenged to serve one another. But that's just what Jesus tells us His way is all about.

How is your attitude toward humbly serving others? Does anything make you reluctant to stoop down—a matter of rank or status, for example, or the type of service or the type of person you need to serve?

_____

_____

_____

_____

_____

Jesus has passed us His towel. If He is really our Lord, then we need to willingly follow in His humble steps. What in your everyday life needs to be transformed by God's amazing humility?

_____

_____

_____

_____

_____

Chapter 11
How High Is Your A.Q.?
John 13:18–30

Leonardo da Vinci's timeless masterpiece, *Last Supper,* captures the dramatic moment when Jesus announces to His disciples that one of them will betray Him.

> Turmoil disrupts the Passover table as the twelve disciples react to Christ's forewarning. In capturing this moment before the traitor is revealed, Leonardo plumbed a psychological depth unknown in previous paintings of the Last Supper.[1]

In the painting, the disciples are grouped in threes, artistically heightening the drama. And in each cluster of three, all the participants are aghast with shock, expressing amazement to one another. All, that is, except Judas.

Recoiling from Jesus' words, Judas clutches a leather pouch . . . the pouch that holds his betrayal fee. Da Vinci ironically depicts him knocking over the salt cellar. One of the men chosen to be the salt of the world is the very one about to rub salt into the Savior's wounds.

In the shadow of his own guilt, Judas clutches more than thirty pieces of silver. He holds tightly in his heart a secret only he and Jesus share at that table: he is the betrayer.

I. Definition of A.Q.
The story of Judas and the Last Supper shows us something magnificent about the Savior and about His ability to accept others in spite of the sin that clings to them. As an I.Q. test measures our minds, indicating our intelligence quotient, an A.Q. test measures our attitudes, indicating our acceptance quotient. In this chapter, we'll take a look at the A.Q. of Jesus with regard to Judas, and then we'll turn the test on our own lives.

   A. Meaning. Our acceptance quotient is our ability to receive another person without inner restrictions of prejudice or outer requirements of performance.

   B. Clarification. Our acceptance quotient does not nullify discernment; nor does it deny depravity. But it does allow for maximum freedom and individuality. There are few examples better than the Last Supper to help guide our thoughts along

---

1. Carlo Bertelli, "Restoration Reveals the Last Supper," *National Geographic* 164 (November 1983), p. 668.

these lines. In John 13:18–30, we find two individuals face-to-face who could not have been more different: Jesus and Judas; the former with an A.Q. of ten, the latter with an A.Q. of zero.

II. Illustration of A.Q.

Just as the name Benedict Arnold has become synonymous with betrayal in American history, so the name Judas is linked with treason in biblical history.

A. Truth about the traitor. Judas was a hypocrite. With his polished exterior, he looked every inch a disciple; within, however, he was a traitor to the core. Looking back on this night years later, John is quick to point an indicting finger in Judas' direction (see v. 2). But at the time, only Jesus knew of this disciple's plot to betray Him (see v. 11). Christ's knowledge of the betrayal was not some sudden piece of information that surfaced at the dinner table; it had been revealed a thousand years earlier in Psalm 41:9, which Jesus quotes here:

"I do not speak of all of you. I know the ones I have chosen; but it is that the Scripture may be fulfilled, 'He who eats my bread has lifted up his heel against Me.'"[2] (John 13:18)

His disciples, however, don't understand what's coming, and the apparent victory of evil forces over their Leader could throw their faith. So Jesus shores up their belief in Him by directly predicting His imminent betrayal. Then He reaffirms their commission and sets up a contrast with Judas, who doesn't receive Him or the One who sent Him.

"From now on I am telling you before it comes to pass, so that when it does occur, you may believe that I am He. Truly, truly, I say to you, he who receives whomever I send receives Me; and he who receives Me receives Him who sent Me." (vv. 19–20)

B. Treatment of the traitor. Verses 21–22 are the verses that inspired da Vinci to paint the *Last Supper*.

When Jesus had said this, He became troubled in spirit, and testified, and said, "Truly, truly, I say to you, that one of you will betray Me." The disciples began looking at one another, at a loss to know of which one He was speaking.

---

2. Eating bread together symbolizes close fellowship. Most commentators interpret "lifted up his heel" as a metaphor derived from the image of a horse's hoof preparing to kick, indicating a hurtful or destructive act. See Leon Morris, *The Gospel according to John,* rev. ed., The New International Commentary on the New Testament Series (Grand Rapids, Mich.: William B. Eerdmans Publishing Co., 1995), p. 553.

The seating arrangement, however, was not quite as da Vinci presented it, as verses 23–26 indicate.

> There was reclining on Jesus' breast one of His disciples, whom Jesus loved. Simon Peter therefore gestured to him, and said to him, "Tell us who it is of whom He is speaking." He, leaning back thus on Jesus' breast, said to Him, "Lord, who is it?" Jesus therefore answered, "That is the one for whom I shall dip the morsel and give it to him." So when He had dipped the morsel, He took and gave it to Judas, the son of Simon Iscariot.

First of all, the Jews did not sit at traditional tables as we know them. Their tables were low, solid blocks with pillows or pallets around them for the guests to recline upon (see v. 23a). They reclined, leaning on the left elbow, leaving the right hand free to eat with. Sitting in such a way, a man's head was quite literally in the breast of the person who was reclining to his left. That would place John, the author of the Gospel, on Jesus' right (see v. 23b). Since it is obvious that Jesus also spoke privately with Judas (see vv. 26–27), most likely that disciple was seated at Jesus' left. William Barclay explains the significance of this.

> The revealing thing is that *the place on the left of the host was the place of highest honour, kept for the most intimate friend.* When that meal began, Jesus must have said to Judas: "Judas, come and sit beside me tonight; I want specially to talk to you." The very inviting of Judas to that seat was an appeal.[3]

C. Change in the traitor. Realizing the power of Jesus' love to soften the heart of even the most mercenary of traitors, Satan steps in to make sure that nothing foils his assassination plot.

> And after the morsel, Satan then entered into him. Jesus therefore said to him, "What you do, do quickly." Now no one of those reclining at the table knew for what purpose He had said this to him. For some were supposing, because Judas had the money box, that Jesus was saying to him, "Buy the things we have need of for the feast"; or else, that he should give something to the poor. (vv. 27–29)

---

3. William Barclay, *The Gospel of John,* rev. ed., The Daily Study Bible Series (Philadelphia, Pa.: Westminster Press, 1975), vol. 2, pp. 145–46.

Remember: acceptance doesn't mean putting a blindfold on discernment or ignoring depravity.

Scripture clearly states that there are times when we are *not* to fellowship with certain people. John implores us, in his second epistle, not to commune closely with anyone involved in cults. In his third epistle he declares that the church cannot tolerate Diotrephes, an errant, self-willed brother. And in 1 Corinthians 5:9–13, Paul clearly teaches us to not only separate ourselves from an immoral believer but actually remove that person from the church (see also 2 Thess. 3:6, 14–15).

There is a time to accept fellowship and a time to reject it. Jesus held out His hand to Judas until he consciously decided to carry out his plan. And we, too, must hold out our hand of fellowship until a person takes that rebellious step outside the doctrinal and moral circle that encloses us.

D. Reaction of the traitor. Like Pharaoh, unbending and unchanged, Judas' heart remains hardened. And so he ventures out into the cold, dark alleyways of betrayal—far from the Light that loved him and offered him warmth.

And so after receiving the morsel he went out immediately; and it was night. (John 13:30)

III. Application of A.Q.

Using this passage as a practical basis of comparison, we want to drive home the importance of a high A.Q. score in three areas.

A. Willingness to accept people without partiality. The subject is prejudice. Look at James 2:1–4.

My brethren, do not hold your faith in our glorious Lord Jesus Christ with an attitude of personal favoritism. For if a man comes into your assembly with a gold ring and dressed in fine clothes, and there also comes in a poor man in dirty clothes, and you pay special attention to the one who is wearing the fine clothes, and say, "You sit here in a good place," and you say to the poor man, "You stand over there, or sit down by my footstool," have you not made distinctions among yourselves, and become judges with evil motives?

The root of preferring one person over another is sin, as James points out later in chapter 2.

> But if you show partiality, you are committing sin and are convicted by the law as transgressors. (v. 9)

How do you respond when somebody who doesn't quite fit the typical membership profile comes to your church? Say the person is poor, with threadbare, unwashed clothes. Or maybe the haircut doesn't make the proper doctrinal statement. What if the person is mentally, physically, or emotionally handicapped? Or divorced? Or a different color . . . or of another political persuasion?

B. **Willingness to accept another style without jealousy or criticism.** No one exemplified this more than Jesus.

> John said to Him, "Teacher, we saw someone casting out demons in Your name, and we tried to hinder him because he was not following us." But Jesus said, "Do not hinder him, for there is no one who shall perform a miracle in My name, and be able soon afterward to speak evil of Me. For he who is not against us is for us." (Mark 9:38–40)

This same emphasis can be seen in Paul's life, whose major concern was to reach the world with the message of the gospel. *How* the world was reached was of significantly lesser concern (see Phil. 1:15–18). Does a pride of style or size characterize your evaluation of churches? Does a pride of philosophy or personality keep you from accepting another church's contribution to the spread of the gospel? Certainly John the Baptist, with his unusual garb and hermit's ways, doesn't fit our mold of evangelist. Yet God used him as the forerunner to His Son.

C. **Willingness to accept offenses without holding a grudge.** Remember, Jesus washed the very heels that were raised against Him . . . and fed a morsel to the very lips that would kiss His cheek to identify Him to His captors. Emulating the example of Christ, Paul exhorts us in Romans 12:14–21:

> Bless those who persecute you; bless and curse not. Rejoice with those who rejoice, and weep with those who weep. Be of the same mind toward one another; do not be haughty in mind, but associate with the lowly. Do not be wise in your own estimation. Never pay back evil for evil to anyone. Respect what is right in the sight of all men. If possible, so far as it depends on you, be at peace with all men. Never take your own revenge, beloved, but leave room for the wrath of God, for it is written, "Vengeance is

Mine, I will repay," says the Lord. "But if your enemy is hungry, feed him, and if he is thirsty, give him a drink; for in so doing you will heap burning coals upon his head." Do not be overcome by evil, but overcome evil with good.

Do you plot how to get even when wronged, or do you truly forgive and forget? Do you look for opportunities to gossip about someone who's offended you, or do you speak well of those who have wounded you with their words? Do you stomp off and leave the class or the church like a spoiled child, or do you stay and try to make peace?

The Fragrance of Forgiveness

It is said that forgiveness is the fragrance the violet sheds on the heel that has crushed it. If so, could there be a fragrance as sweet in all the Bible as that of Jesus washing the feet of the very one whose heel was raised against Him?

Many things have been said against Christ, but He has never been accused of not practicing what He preached. And Jesus' last moments with His betrayer are a perfect example of His exhortation to "love your enemies, and pray for those who persecute you" (Matt. 5:44). This He did even to the end, when He hung on that cross and prayed: "Father, forgive them; for they do not know what they are doing" (Luke 23:34).

How do you respond when a heel of betrayal comes crushing down on you? No one relishes being stepped on, any more than a violet does. But when it happens, let the example of Jesus guide your response. Let His fragrance exude in you a potent forgiveness, reaching the nostrils of the one whose heel has hurt you.

 Living Insights

What a powerful model of love and acceptance Jesus is to us! Let's allow His example to inspire us as well as shine a light on areas where we need to emulate Him more closely.

How willing are you to accept other people without partiality? Did any of the questions asked in that section of this chapter strike a nerve with you? Which ones? What is going on in your heart?

_____

_____

_____

_____

_____

_____

_____

What do you need to do to follow more in Jesus' gracious footsteps?

_____

_____

_____

_____

_____

How accepting are you of another person's style? Of another ministry's style? Of another denomination's style? Take a moment to listen to your own opinions. How open and welcoming are they? How critical and rejecting are they? Do they reflect God's love for all His people?

_____

_____

_____

_____

_____

What do you need to do to leave more judgments with God?

_____

_____

_____

_____

_____

_____

_____

_____

Here's a tough one: How are you doing with people who have offended or hurt you? What is normally your first response? Revenge, gossip, or rejection? Or a movement toward forgiveness, truth, and seeking peace?

_____

_____

_____

_____

_____

_____

_____

What do you need to do to better reflect Christ's forgiveness?

_____

_____

_____

_____

_____

_____

_____

Chapter 12
Agapē . . . Authentic Love
John 13:31–38

In his book *The Mark of a Christian,* Dr. Francis Schaeffer discusses the quality that distinctively sets believers apart as children of God. It is not a pithy bumper sticker or an *ichthus* dangling from the neck or a gilded dove pinned on the lapel. These are only symbols of our faith. The true mark of the Christian is love.

Arthur Pink, in his commentary on John, says it well:

> Love is the *badge* of Christian discipleship. It is not knowledge, nor orthodoxy, nor fleshly activities, but (supremely) *love* which identifies a follower of the Lord Jesus. As the disciples of the Pharisees were known by their phylacteries, as the disciples of John were known by their baptism, and every school by its particular shibboleth, so the mark of a true Christian is *love*; and that, a genuine, active love, not in words but in deeds.[1]

In John 13, Jesus gives His eleven true disciples a mandate that adds a new dimension to the meaning of love. And this new dimension not only changes lives but, in a compelling way, shows the world that we belong to Jesus.

I. Jesus and the Disciples

In verses 31–35, Jesus discusses two main topics: His departure and His command to the disciples.

A. His departure. In our last lesson, we left the disciples gathered with Jesus at a final meal together. As soon as Judas leaves, Jesus speaks of another departure—His own.

> When therefore he had gone out, Jesus said, "Now is the Son of Man glorified, and God is glorified in Him; if God is glorified in Him, God will also glorify Him in Himself, and will glorify Him immediately." (vv. 31–32)

Five times in this passage Jesus uses some form of the word *glorify.* For Him, death is not a mournful tragedy but a magnificent triumph. It is glorious, not gruesome. That is heaven's vantage point (compare Ps. 116:15). Jesus knows that His

---

1. Arthur Pink, *Exposition of the Gospel of John* (Grand Rapids, Mich.: Zondervan Publishing House, 1968), vol. 1, p. 341.

teaching is difficult for the disciples to understand, so He patiently assures them by tenderly expressing His paternal care for them.

> "Little children,[2] I am with you a little while longer. You shall seek Me; and as I said to the Jews, I now say to you also, 'Where I am going, you cannot come.'" (v. 33)

Jesus shifts His tone in verse 33. He no longer speaks in mystical shades of meaning, but becomes very explicit. In doing so, He presents the puzzled disciples with three hard facts they would have to face: first, His departure is imminent; second, people will look for Him and be confused; and third, nobody can come with Him—including the eleven. There's a distinct finality in Jesus' words, which poses an enormous problem for the disciples: How will they go on? With their Master gone, what will be their identity? Won't they lose their impact?

B. His command. Anticipating their insecurity, Jesus stabilizes His disciples with a weighty command.

> "A new commandment I give to you, that you love one another, even as I have loved you, that you also love one another. By this all men will know that you are My disciples, if you have love for one another." (vv. 34–35)

In these verses Jesus not only commands a new dynamic, He predicts a new impact as well.

1. The dynamic. The first thing to note about Jesus' command is that He terms it "new." It is not simply additional or different, it is fresh and unique, as Leon Morris explains:

> Jesus is not speaking here of love to all people but of love within the community of believers. . . . Love itself is not a new commandment, but an old one (Lev. 19:18). The new thing appears to be the mutual affection that Christians have for one another on account of Christ's great love for them. . . . Jesus himself has set the example. He calls on them now to follow in his steps.[3]

---

2. "Little children" is a term expressing affection that is found only once in this Gospel. Other than in this reference, the phrase is seen only seven times in the New Testament, all in 1 John.

3. Leon Morris, *The Gospel According to John*, rev. ed., The New International Commentary on the New Testament Series (Grand Rapids, Mich.: William B. Eerdmans Publishing Co., 1995), p. 562.

The word Jesus uses in verse 35 is *agapē*. Of the Greeks' four words for love, this one is the capstone. Essentially, it means to seek the highest good of another.[4] This type of love refuses to respond negatively, refuses to reject, refuses to demand conditions, and refuses to nitpick the lint off someone's soul. When Jesus says, "as I have loved you," He sets Himself up as the standard by which they are to forever measure their love for one another. He is telling them, "I left the splendors and comforts of heaven because I loved you. I called you to be Mine, knowing full well your faults. I taught you, even when you were stubborn and closed-minded. I corrected you when you stepped out of line. I washed your feet on the way to My death. All this was for your highest good. My interest was not in Myself, but in you."

2. **The impact.** In a word: incredible. It extends to all people (v. 35). Nobody can ignore authentic love. Nothing is more impressive than unselfish attention. The word *know* in verse 35 does not refer to theoretical knowledge but to knowledge gained by firsthand, rub-of-the-shoulders observation. And what will these observers know? That we belong to Jesus! Our love for each other will be a distinctive badge of His ownership. An *ichthus* links us to a belief . . . a cross links us to a religion . . . but love links us to Jesus Himself. That's the mark that matters— the mark that makes a difference.

A Quote to Consider

"It is probably impossible to love any human being simply 'too much.' We may love him too much *in proportion* to our love for God; but it is the smallness of our love for God, not the greatness of our love for the man, that constitutes the inordinacy."[5]

II. Jesus and Simon Peter

Apparently, Christ's words about His departure hit Peter like a two-by-four, because he completely misses the new commandment.

A. Destiny questioned. Look closely at Peter's remark.

Simon Peter said to Him, "Lord, where are You

---

4. For a more detailed analysis of agapē love, see 1 Corinthians 13:4–8a. For an example of this love, see Philippians 2:3–8.

5. C. S. Lewis, *The Four Loves* (New York, N.Y.: Harcourt Brace Jovanovich, 1960), p. 170.

going?" Jesus answered, "Where I go, you cannot follow Me now; but you shall follow later." Peter said to Him, "Lord, why can I not follow You right now?" (vv. 36–37a)

It is obvious from his remarks that Peter is interested not only in Jesus' leaving but also in his being left behind.

B. Loyalty declared. In an impulsive but improvident expression of sincerity, Peter declares his undying allegiance to Jesus.

"I will lay down my life for You." (v. 37b)

C. Reality predicted. With the sharp edge of reality, Jesus lightly touches the surface of Peter's loyalty—a touch that draws blood.

Jesus answered, "Will you lay down your life for Me? Truly, truly, I say to you, a cock shall not crow, until you deny Me three times." (v. 38)

III. Jesus and You

From this passage we can glean three truths about how our love should be expressed to other Christians.

A. Authentic love is unconditional in its expression. There are no *ifs* attached to authentic love . . . no threats . . . no demands. Do you exhibit this type of love to your spouse? How about to your children? Or do you withhold your love until they've lived up to your standards? Do they feel unconditionally loved, or do they feel they're constantly trying to gain your acceptance?

B. Authentic love is unselfish in its motive. Remember Paul's words: Love "is not jealous . . . does not seek its own" (1 Cor. 13:4–5). Love does not manipulate to get its way. Love always looks after number two—not exclusively after number one (see Phil. 2:3–4). How about you? When you show love to someone else, is it weighed in the balance of what you will receive in return? True love gives—with no thought of getting anything in return.

C. Authentic love is unlimited in its benefits. When you love unconditionally and unselfishly, you always walk away the winner. Not only are others built up and encouraged, but so are you! Of course, when you love this way, you become vulnerable. But if you never step out on a limb with people, you'll never grasp the fruit of nourishing relationships.

┌─ *A Final Thought* ─────────────────────────────

"To love at all is to be vulnerable. Love anything, and your heart will certainly be wrung and possibly be broken. If you want to make sure of keeping it intact, you must give your heart to no one, not even to an animal.

Wrap it carefully round with hobbies and little luxuries; avoid all entanglements; lock it up safe in the casket or coffin of your selfishness. But in that casket—safe, dark, motionless, airless—it will change. It will not be broken; it will become unbreakable, impenetrable, irredeemable."[6]

Living Insights

What does biblical love look like? Look up the following passages and write down God's own description of love expressed.

John 15:13 _____

Romans 12:9–21 _____

_____

_____

_____

_____

Romans 13:10, Matthew 7:12, and Galatians 5:14 _____

_____

_____

1 Corinthians 13:4–7 _____

_____

_____

_____

Galatians 5:13 _____

_____

Ephesians 4:2 _____

_____

6. Lewis, *The Four Loves,* p. 169.

Ephesians 4:15, 25 _____

_____

Ephesians 4:32 _____

_____

Philippians 2:3–5 _____

_____

_____

Colossians 3:14 _____

_____

1 Timothy 1:5 _____

_____

1 Peter 1:22; 4:8 _____

_____

1 John 2:5 _____

_____

1 John 3:16–18 _____

_____

1 John 4:18 _____

_____

The apostle Paul wrote to the Thessalonians, "Now as to the love of the brethren, you have no need for anyone to write to you, for you yourselves are taught by God to love one another; for indeed you do practice it toward all . . ." (1 Thess. 4:9–10a). In what areas and ways are you excelling at loving your neighbor as yourself (see James 2:8)?

_____

_____

_____

_____

_____

_____

_____

In what areas and ways would you like to "excel still more" (1 Thess. 4:10b)?

_____

_____

_____

_____

_____

_____

Remember, love is to be the Christian's mark of distinction. So spend some time this week thinking about how you can "stimulate one another to love and good deeds" (Heb. 10:24). If you need help getting started, check out another writing of our Gospel writer, 1 John. This five-chapter letter is simple, profound, and challenging!

Chapter 13

Tranquil Words for
Troubled Hearts

John 14:1–24

For the prodigal son, who left his family and squandered his inheritance in indulgent, immoral living, home was a faraway place. Yet thoughts of home tugged at his heart like a magnet to steel and brought him to his senses. Returning home, he found embracing arms, robes and rings, fatted calves, music and dancing. There he found acceptance, restoration, fellowship, and joy. There he found a tranquil haven for his troubled heart.

Our homes are designed to be a hint of heaven, the dim glimmer of a more beautiful, more secure, more peaceful place. J. Howard Payne wrote fondly of this in the poem "Home Sweet Home."

> 'Mid pleasures and palaces though
> we may roam,
> Be it ever so humble, there's no place
> like Home.[1]

Payne's words conjure up images of the 1939 movie *The Wizard of Oz,* where Dorothy awakes from her harrowing adventures in the fantasy world of Oz, repeating over and over: "There's no place like home." Troubled by her dream, Dorothy takes comfort in being home—safe in her own bed, cuddled by her own blanket, surrounded by her own family and friends. Kansas and Auntie Em never looked so good!

For Christians, our pilgrimage here on earth is like Dorothy's journey down the Yellow Brick Road. It is filled with illusory dreams, frightening experiences, and disappointing realities, in spite of our hopes. And the farther we travel down that road, the more our intuitive self insists that this is not our home; heaven is.

In John 14, Jesus senses the troubled hearts within His disciples and calms them with tranquil words—words that turn their thoughts toward home.

---

1. As quoted in *Five Thousand Quotations for All Occasions,* ed. Lewis C. Henry (Garden City, N.Y.: Doubleday and Co., 1945), p. 123.

I. Thoughts That Trouble the Heart

The chapter break between John 13:38, where we ended the last lesson, and 14:1, where we start this study, is abrupt and unfortunate because it leaves us without sufficient background to the passage. Contextually, the words of Jesus in chapter 14 answer Peter's question in 13:36–37 which, in turn, refers back to Jesus' statement about His departure in verse 33. This explains why the disciples are troubled (14:1, 27). Let's take a closer look at the thoughts that have troubled not only their hearts but ours as well.

A. **Thoughts regarding death.** Jesus had told the disciples He would die soon (13:33a), causing them to be afraid. The fear of death, either our own or a loved one's, troubles our lives like a hurricane sweeping over a serene harbor. Anchored in the shallows, our little boats of faith are easily dashed against the rocks by fear's fury.

B. **Thoughts regarding trials.** Jesus then told His disciples that they could not come with Him when He would leave (v. 33b). This confusing trial made them anxious and frustrated. For us, daily living takes its toll. We tear our hair out or bite our nails to the nub over the day-to-day tempests that blow through our lives. But for all our worry, we are left with only a handful of hair where there could have been character, and ten throbbing fingers where there could have been faith.

C. **Thoughts regarding disloyalty.** Upon hearing Peter's strong pledge of loyalty (vv. 36–37), Jesus predicted his impending denial (v. 38). Disobedience and disloyalty always produce guilt. Like Peter, all of us have denied Christ in some way or another. If we haven't denied Him with words, then we have in deeds. And if not in deeds, then certainly in thoughts.

II. Truths That Quiet the Heart

The first twenty verses of chapter 14 link together a chain of counsel so strong and secure that it will help us weather even the most inclement of circumstances.

A. **Personal faith in a personal God brings personal strength.**
    "Let not your heart be troubled; believe in God,
    believe also in Me." (v. 1)
The verbs are present imperatives, with the sense of: "Keep on believing in God . . . keep on believing in Me." The disciples had trusted Jesus to put them in the boat of salvation; now they must trust Him to bring them through the storm and safely to harbor. Every test that blows our way can either fill our sails with faith or break our mast from the strain of unbelief.

B. While preparing a place for us, Christ is preparing us for that place.

"In My Father's house are many dwelling places;[2] if it were not so, I would have told you; for I go to prepare a place for you. And if I go and prepare a place for you, I will come again, and receive you to Myself; that where I am, there you may be also. And you know the way where I am going." (vv. 2–4)

As God fashions us for heaven, the tools He uses most often are trials and troubles (see Rom. 5:3–4). Pressures are part of the process of making us perfect and complete, as James informs us.

Consider it all joy, my brethren, when you encounter various trials, knowing that the testing of your faith produces endurance. And let endurance have its perfect result, that you may be perfect and complete, lacking in nothing. (1:2–4)

Jesus' claim in John 14:4 prompts a question from the empirical mind of Thomas: "Lord, we do not know where You are going, how do we know the way?" (v. 5). To which Jesus answers:

"I am the way, and the truth, and the life; no one comes to the Father, but through Me." (v. 6)

The Living Way

Imagine yourself asking for directions in a strange town. Suppose the other person says: "Take the first left here and go left at the second intersection. Turn right at the second street and go left when it makes a Y, and then go right." Chances are you'll get lost halfway there.

But suppose that person says: "Follow me. I'll take you there." In that case, the person *is* the way. And that's precisely the case with Jesus. He doesn't point the way in the distance or draw us some impersonal map. He takes us by the hand and leads us. If you're lost, or if

---

2. "The Greek word *monē* . . . properly signifies a 'dwelling place.' Because the Latin Vulgate rendered it *mansiones*, the AV/KJV, followed by the RV used 'mansions.' However, since heaven is here pictured as the Father's *house*, it is more natural to think of 'dwelling-places' within a house as *rooms* (NIV) or suites or the like. . . . The point is not the lavishness of each apartment, but the fact that such ample provision has been made that there is more than enough space for every one of Jesus' disciples to join him in his Father's home." D. A. Carson, *The Gospel according to John* (Grand Rapids, Mich.: William B. Eerdmans Publishing Co., 1991), pp. 488–89.

you've played the prodigal and simply strayed, Jesus is the way home to the Father—the *only* way. Won't you place your hand in His and let Him lead you there?

C. The sovereign hand of God is at work. Jesus continues trying to console the troubled hearts of His disciples, but they still have difficulty following His deeply profound line of thinking.

"If you had known Me, you would have known My father also; from now on you know Him, and have seen Him." Philip said to Him, "Lord, show us the Father, and it is enough for us." Jesus said to him, "Have I been so long with you, and yet you have not come to know Me, Philip? He who has seen Me has seen the Father; how do you say, 'Show us the Father'? Do you not believe that I am in the Father, and the Father is in Me? The words that I say to you I do not speak on My own initiative, but the Father abiding in Me does His works. Believe Me that I am in the Father, and the Father in Me; otherwise believe on account of the works themselves." (vv. 7–11)

Jesus has said repeatedly that the Father has sent Him, that He speaks only what the Father tells Him, that He does what the Father shows Him to do, and that He and the Father are one.[3] He has even said that anyone "who beholds Me beholds the One who sent Me" (12:45). Jesus shows us what God is like, and how often we, like Philip, miss it. Also, notice how completely God was in charge of Jesus' life and how Jesus welcomed His sovereignty. God is sovereignly in charge of our lives too—only we don't acknowledge and rest in this truth as well as Jesus did. When troubling circumstances disturb our hearts, we need to remember that God is working in us through them, refining us and shaping us into the glorious image of His own Son (compare 1 Pet. 1:6–9).

D. Greater things occur when we pray in Jesus' name, that the Father may be glorified.

"Truly, truly, I say to you, he who believes in Me, the works that I do shall he do also; and greater works than these shall he do; because I go to the Father. And whatever you ask in My name, that will I do,

---

3. See John 5:17, 19–23, 30, 36–37a, 43; 6:38, 57; 7:16–18, 28–29; 8:16–18, 28–29, 42; 10:14–15, 30, 36–38; 11:42; 12:44–45, 49–50; 13:20. Clearly, this was a key theme in Jesus' ministry.

Thursday	September 7	**Seeking before Hiding**
		John 12
Friday	September 8	**Seeking before Hiding**

Monday	September 11	**Humility Personified**
		John 13:1–17
Tuesday	September 12	**Humility Personified**
Wednesday	September 13	**How High Is Your A.Q.?**
		John 13:18–30
Thursday	September 14	**How High Is Your A.Q.?**
Friday	September 15	**Agapé . . . Authentic Love**
		John 13:31–38

Monday	September 18	**Agapé . . . Authentic Love**
Tuesday	September 19	**Tranquil Words for Troubled Hearts**
		John 14:1–24
Wednesday	September 20	**Tranquil Words for Troubled Hearts**
Thursday	September 21	**Overcoming Fear**
		John 14:25–31
Friday	September 22	**Overcoming Fear**

Broadcast schedule is subject to change without notice.

Insight for Living • Post Office Box 69000, Anaheim, CA 92817-0900
Insight for Living Ministries • Post Office Box 2510, Vancouver, BC, Canada V6B 3W7
Insight for Living, Inc. • 20 Albert Street, Blackburn, VIC 3130, Australia
Printed in the United States of America

INSIGHT FOR LIVING

—— Broadcast Schedule ——

Following Christ . . . The Man of God
A Study of John 5–14

August 16–September 22, 2000

Wednesday	**August 16**	**God's Speciality: Impossibilities** *John 6:1–21*
Thursday	**August 17**	**God's Speciality: Impossibilities**
Friday	**August 18**	**Bread Delivered from Heaven** *John 6:22–71*

Monday	**August 21**	**Bread Delivered from Heaven**
Tuesday	**August 22**	**Jesus in the Lions' Den** *John 7*
Wednesday	**August 23**	**Jesus in the Lions' Den**
Thursday	**August 24**	**Letters in the Sand** *John 8:1–11*
Friday	**August 25**	**Letters in the Sand**

Monday	**August 28**	**Reasons for Rejection** *John 8:12–59*
Tuesday	**August 29**	**Reasons for Rejection**
Wednesday	**August 30**	**Blind Men's Bluff** *John 9*
Thursday	**August 31**	**Blind Men's Bluff**
Friday	**September 1**	**The Living Door** *John 10*

Monday	**September 4**	**The Living Door**
Tuesday	**September 5**	**Back from Beyond** *John 11*
Wednesday	**September 6**	**Back from Beyond**

that the Father may be glorified in the Son. If you
ask Me anything in My name, I will do it." (vv. 12–14)
Like Aladdin's lamp, these verses have suffered centuries of
misuse. All too often, Christ has been looked on as a magic
genie; and prayer, the fervent rub to the lamp. So many times,
our prayers are like a stanza from "Old MacDonald's Farm":
"a gimme gimme here and a gimme gimme there . . . here a
gimme . . . there a gimme . . . everywhere a gimme gimme."
But the verse is not a carte blanche to gratify our every desire.
Notice that our preface to prayer should be "in My name" and
our purpose for prayer is "that the Father may be glorified in
the Son" (v. 13).

E. **You are not alone; you have an inward Helper.** For the first
time, Jesus informs His troubled disciples about the Holy Spirit.

"And I will ask the Father, and He will give you
another Helper,[4] that He may be with you forever;
that is the Spirit of truth, whom the world cannot
receive, because it does not behold Him or know
Him, but you know Him because He abides with
you, and will be in you. I will not leave you as orphans; I will come to you." (vv. 16–18)

The thought that devastates us most is that we're alone . . .
that nobody understands, or cares. As Christians, however,
we never have to fear that. For within us dwells infinite comfort and care in the person of the Holy Spirit.

F. **Your life is inseparably linked to Christ Himself.**

"After a little while the world will behold Me no more;
but you will behold Me; because I live, you shall
live also. In that day you shall know that I am in My
Father, and you in Me, and I in you." (vv. 19–20)

The world lives by sight, and when Jesus is out of sight, He's
out of mind. But Christians live by faith (2 Cor. 5:7) and see
the eternal dimension of Christ behind their circumstances.
We have the confidence that whatever circumstances befall

---

4. *Paraklētos* means "called to one's aid," or as William Barclay explains, "It really means
someone who is called in; but it is the reason *why* the person is called in which gives the word
its distinctive associations. The Greeks used the word in a wide variety of ways. A *paraklētos*
might be a person *called in* to give witness in a law court in someone's favour; he might be
an advocate *called in* to plead the cause of someone under a charge which would issue in
serious penalty; he might be an expert *called in* to give advice in some difficult situation; he
might be a person *called in* when, for example, a company of soldiers were depressed and
dispirited to put new courage into their minds and hearts. Always a *paraklētos* is *someone
called in to help* in time of trouble or need." William Barclay, *The Gospel of John*, rev. ed., The
Daily Study Bible Series (Philadelphia, Pa.: Westminster Press, 1975), vol. 2, pp. 166–67.

us, they can work together for the good of conforming us to Christ's image (Rom. 8:28–29).

Training the Eye to See

Our ability to see is influenced largely by what we have been trained to look for. A doctor will see more by looking down the throat of a sick child than any parent could. An artist will appreciate a tour through a gallery much more than someone without those sensibilities. A seamstress will appreciate a finely tailored outfit much more than someone whose eyes have not been trained to notice such subtleties of style and precision.

So, too, if our eyes are trained to see God's hand in our circumstances, then each pressure indenting the clay of our lives will be seen not to bend us out of shape but to mold us into vessels of honor—fit for a King.

III. Techniques That Strengthen the Heart

In John 14:21–24 we find three principles that will strengthen our weak hearts.

"He who has My commandments and keeps them, he it is who loves Me; and he who loves Me shall be loved by My Father, and I will love him, and will disclose Myself to him." Judas (not Iscariot) said to Him, "Lord, what then has happened that You are going to disclose Yourself to us, and not to the world?" Jesus answered and said to him, "If anyone loves Me, he will keep My word; and My Father will love him, and We will come to him, and make Our abode with him. He who does not love Me does not keep My words; and the word which you hear is not Mine, but the Father's who sent Me."

First, *knowledge of the truth removes fear* (v. 20). It's remarkable how information from God's Word takes away the superstition and trauma of death. Second, *application of the knowledge reduces anxiety.* Note the phrase "he who has my commandments and keeps them" (v. 21). That means making God's Word a vital part of our lives. Third, *love for the Lord releases guilt* (vv. 23–24). Love is the highest of motivations, and when we love the Lord, we desire to please Him (2 Cor. 5:9).

At the beginning of this chapter, Jesus calmed the disciples with words about His Father's house. If that is not enough to still your troubled heart, Jesus spoke more tranquil words at the end of our passage. He said that while you remain on earth in your temporary tent (2 Cor. 5:1), He and the Father will make their home in your heart and dwell in it (John 14:23). Just as the glory of the Lord filled the tabernacle in the wilderness, so the Trinity will fill your heart with their majestic presence. And that light residing in you is sufficient to dispel even the darkest and most foreboding of shadows!

Living Insights

"Let not your heart be troubled," Jesus tells us (John 14:1a). Is anything troubling your heart today? What is it?

_____

_____

_____

_____

_____

_____

How has this impacted your ability to believe in Jesus and the promises the Father sent Him to deliver (v. 2)? Have you been able to cling to Him in faith, taking your fears, worries, and sorrows to Him? Or have you felt too confused and discouraged to trust the Lord with your troubles?

_____

_____

_____

_____

_____

_____

_____

Too often, the limits of our understanding impair our ability to reach out—with even a shaky hand—in faith. Then, when we don't reach out in faith, we can't grasp the comfort the Lord is holding out for us. And Jesus has so much He wants to give us. To bolster your belief during those times when your heart just wants to give out, review what Jesus is providing for you and remind yourself of His promises of everlasting care and compassion.

John 14:2 _____

v. 3 _____

v. 6 _____

v. 13 _____

v. 16 _____

v. 18 _____

v. 19 _____

v. 21 _____

v. 23 _____

Remember, Jesus gave these promises only hours before He would endure the horrors of the Cross. And where was His attention? On comforting others and reassuring them of His eternal love. That's a Lord our hearts can rest in, no matter what.

> "Peace I leave with you; My peace I give to you; not as the world gives, do I give to you. Let not your heart be troubled, nor let it be fearful. . . . These things I have spoken to you, that in Me you may have peace. In the world you have tribulation, but take courage; I have overcome the world." (14:27; 16:33)

Chapter 14

Overcoming Fear

John 14:25–31

Earlier in his Gospel, John recounted a dramatic story of overcoming fear (6:16–21).

The disciples had piled into a boat to row across the Sea of Galilee. A calm settled over the waters that moonless evening—a calm that was shattered by merciless winds. Like a woman in the throes of childbirth, the sea swelled with undulating momentum. And with every contraction, their small boat yawed in helpless response.

The disciples rowed even more furiously. But blinded by stinging whips of seawater, they realized the utter futility of their desperate efforts. And within, their fears raged in velocity equal to that of the wind and waves around them.

Then they looked up—Jesus was walking toward them. "It is I," He said. "Do not be afraid." And that's all it took to alleviate their fears. Suddenly the sea became quiet, and they found themselves safely on shore.

In this chapter, fear is the focal point. Like the Sea of Galilee's thrashing waves, fear loomed over the disciples on the night before Jesus' death. It surrounded them. Overwhelmed them. But just as Jesus had quieted their fears and calmed the storm with His presence, so He promised the presence of another who would do the same when He was gone.

I. When Did Fear Originate?

Fear is an instinct literally as old as Adam.

A. The first appearance of fear. The creeping vine of fear entered Eden through the gates of the Fall. When Adam and Eve disobeyed God and ate the forbidden fruit, fear entwined itself around their hearts.

> When the woman saw that the tree was good for food, and that it was a delight to the eyes, and that the tree was desirable to make one wise, she took from its fruit and ate; and she gave also to her husband with her, and he ate. Then the eyes of both of them were opened, and they knew that they were naked; and they sewed fig leaves together and made themselves loin coverings. And they heard the sound of the Lord God walking in the garden in the cool of the day, and the man and his wife hid themselves from the presence of the Lord God among

the trees of the garden. Then the Lord God called to the man, and said to him, "Where are you?" And he said, "I heard the sound of Thee in the garden, *and I was afraid* because I was naked; so I hid myself." (Gen. 3:6–10, emphasis added)

B. The first result of fear. When Adam and Eve sinned, they suddenly became self-conscious, covering themselves with fig leaves. Like veneer covers particle board with a coat of acceptability, the fig leaves served to hide their splintered relationship with God. Cover-ups began with the Fall and have been used to hide guilt ever since.

II. Why Did Fear Occur?

Upon hearing of Christ's imminent death and their inability to go with Him (John 13:33), the disciples found themselves in a swirling vortex of confusion (14:5, 22). But just as they were about to go under, Jesus threw them a lifeline: "Let not your heart be troubled, nor let it be fearful" (v. 27b). Jesus' words are important—they imply that the disciples had the ability to control the reactions of their hearts. And if they could keep their emotions afloat during the tempests they experienced, maybe there's hope for us as well.

III. How Is Fear Overcome?

In verses 25–31, we find four distinct means of power to abate fear's consuming undertow.

A. Depending on the person of the Holy Spirit. Verses 25–26 reveal that the Holy Spirit will buoy us up in Christ's absence.

"These things I have spoken to you, while abiding with you. But the Helper, the Holy Spirit, whom the Father will send in My name, He will teach you all things, and bring to your remembrance all that I said to you."

Underscore the word *all* in verse 26: "all things . . . all that I said." Teaching and reminding are two of the Holy Spirit's ministries, as 1 Corinthians 2:10–12 notes.

For to us God revealed them through the Spirit; for the Spirit searches all things, even the depths of God. For who among men knows the thoughts of a man except the spirit of the man, which is in him? Even so the thoughts of God no one knows except the Spirit of God. Now we have received, not the spirit of the world, but the Spirit who is from God, that we might know the things freely given to us by God.

"How does this relate to fear?" you may ask. Well, we are usually overcome by fear because we either *ignore* or *forget* what God has said. And the Holy Spirit's ministry bridges that important information gap, giving us insight and recall. John reiterates this in his first epistle.

> And as for you, the anointing which you received from Him abides in you, and you have no need for anyone to teach you; but as His anointing teaches you about all things, and is true and is not a lie, and just as it has taught you, you abide in Him. (1 John 2:27)

B. Claiming the peace of Jesus Christ. In John 14:27, Jesus promises the disciples peace to calm their troubled hearts.

> "Peace I leave with you; My peace I give to you; not as the world gives, do I give to you. Let not your heart be troubled, nor let it be fearful."

The peace Christ promises is not the power of positive thinking. It is not feelings the disciples have to conjure up or circumstances they have to cover up. It is a legacy: "Peace I leave *with* you" (emphasis added). And it is a treasure: "My peace I give *to* you" (emphasis added). Jesus' definition of peace is not the same as the world's—tranquil circumstances. Rather, it is an inner calm in the midst of tempestuous outer storms.

> "These things I have spoken to you, that in Me you may have peace. In the world you have tribulation, but take courage; I have overcome the world." (16:33)

Commentator William Barclay elaborates on the richness of Christ's gift of peace.

> In the Bible the word for *peace, shalōm,* never means simply the absence of trouble. It means everything which makes for our highest good. The peace which the world offers us is the peace of escape, the peace which comes from the avoidance of trouble and from refusing to face things. The peace which Jesus offers us is the peace of conquest. No experience of life can ever take it from us and no sorrow, no danger, no suffering can ever make it less.[1]

This type of peace is foreign to the wicked, in whose souls rage a hurricane of heartache.

> But the wicked are like the tossing sea,
> For it cannot be quiet,
> And its waters toss up refuse and mud.
> "There is no peace," says my God, "for the wicked."
> (Isa. 57:20–21)

---

1. William Barclay, *The Gospel of John*, rev. ed., The Daily Study Bible Series (Philadelphia, Pa.: Westminster Press, 1975), vol. 2, p. 171.

C. Accepting the plan of the future. Jesus had informed the disciples of His planned departure (John 13:33; 14:2–3), but they had trouble accepting it. Verses 28–29 of chapter 14 tell why.

> "You heard that I said to you, 'I go away, and I will come to you.' If you loved Me, you would have rejoiced, because I go to the Father; for the Father is greater than I. And now I have told you before it comes to pass, that when it comes to pass, you may believe."

Bruce Milne explains that in these verses, Jesus

> invites them to rise above what his departure is going to mean for them, to consider what it will mean *for him*. . . . Their love for Jesus should allow them to be happy *for him* that he is going away, since that journey, albeit through the horrors of the cross, will take him again to the intimacy of the Father's bosom, and to the "glory I had with you before the world began" (17:5).[2]

Jesus had His eyes on the everlasting joy that would be His when redemption was accomplished and death would be swallowed up in victory (see Heb. 12:2; 1 Cor. 15:54). And He wanted His disciples to focus their eyes of faith on that too.

D. Following the pattern of obedience. Even facing death and Satan himself, Jesus exudes a calm that sets an example for the disciples—and for us.

> "I will not speak much more with you, for the ruler of the world is coming, and he has nothing in Me; but that the world may know that I love the Father, and as the Father gave Me commandment, even so I do. Arise, let us go from here." (John 14:30–31)

In verse 31, Christ's love for the Father is in sharp relief. Obedience, motivated by love, gives Jesus a warm blanket of peace in the midst of the chilling storm front beginning to roll into His life. And His obedience sets the perfect pattern for us when we find ourselves left alone in a torrential downpour of fateful circumstances.

When the Waves Get Rough

Though the wind and waves obey Him, Christ may not calm all the outer storms in your life. But He can

---

2. Bruce Milne, *The Message of John: Here Is Your King!,* The Bible Speaks Today Series (Downers Grove, Ill.: InterVarsity Press, 1993), pp. 217–18.

take your fearful heart and transform it into a calm, inner eye of faith in the midst of those storms. First, however, you must learn to trust Him.

"The steadfast of mind Thou wilt keep in
perfect peace,
Because he trusts in Thee." (Isa. 26:3)

If you're floundering in this area, here are some practical suggestions that will help anchor you: (1) Acknowledge Jesus Christ as your source of power. (2) Begin your day with prayer and claim His peace. (3) Correct any habits of pessimism by mooring yourself to His prophetic Word. (4) Devote yourself to obedience.

As the Prince of Peace, Jesus merits not only your trust but your obedience as well—even when those waves get rough.

Living Insights

As a final exercise to close this study guide, look over John 6–14 one more time, and take special note of major events in Christ's life.[3] In each case, look carefully at how Jesus responds to situations and problems that come up.

Determine specific aspects of Christ's character, seen in His responses to these situations, that you can imitate. Watch how He avoids further discord by choosing not to respond in ways that would normally be expected from you or me, and mark the differences. As you review, write your observations below. Pray that God would enable you to live more like Christ, following Him as your model—the Man of God.

Observations of Christ's Character

_____

_____

_____

_____

_____

3. This Living Insight has been taken from the original study guide *Following Christ . . . The Man of God*, coauthored by Ken Gire, with Living Insights by Bill Butterworth, from the Bible-teaching ministry of Charles R. Swindoll (Fullerton, Calif.: Insight for Living, 1987), p. 97.

Books for Probing Further

"I am the good shepherd; the good shepherd lays down His life for the sheep" (John 10:11).

Jesus is the Good Shepherd.
His sheep shall not want.
He maketh the five thousand lie down in green pastures
    and feedeth them.
He leadeth His disciples beside the still waters of humility
    and washeth their feet.
He restoreth love to the soul of an adulterous woman,
            light to the eyes of a man born blind,
            life to a dead Lazarus.
With rod and staff He watches over His sheep,
            protecting them,
            assuring them,
            comforting them.
Until at last, the pharisaical wolves
            pack together,
            close in,
            and corner the Good Shepherd.
But in the face of sharp, angry teeth,
            bared for the kill,
            He stands His ground.
And with crimson love,
Lays down His life
For the sheep.   —Ken Gire

As the Good Shepherd, Jesus not only died for His sheep, He lived for them as well, nourishing them with His teaching and healing their wounds with His love. To further nourish you in your study of the Gospel of John, we recommend the following books that tie in to the subjects we've covered. You may also want to consult the books listed in the first volume of Insight for Living's study of John, *Beholding Christ . . . the Son of God.*

I. Jesus Christ

Gariepy, Henry. *100 Portraits of Christ.* Wheaton, Ill.: Scripture Press Publications, Victor Books, 1993.

Gire, Ken. *Incredible Moments with the Savior.* Grand Rapids, Mich.: Zondervan Publishing House, 1990.

Griffiths, Michael. *The Example of Jesus.* The Jesus Library Series. Downers Grove, Ill.: InterVarsity Press, 1985.

II. The Holy Spirit

Brown, Steve W. *Follow the Wind: Our Lord, the Holy Spirit.* Grand Rapids, Mich.: Baker Book House, 1999.

Swindoll, Charles R. *Flying Closer to the Flame.* Dallas, Tex.: Word Publishing, 1993.

Tozer, A. W. *The Counselor.* Camp Hill, Pa.: Christian Publications, 1993.

III. Commentaries

Barton, Bruce B., Philip W. Comfort, David R. Veerman, and Neil Wilson. *John.* Life Application Bible Commentary Series. Wheaton, Ill.: Tyndale House Publishers, 1993.

Hendriksen, William. *Exposition of the Gospel According to John.* Two volumes in one. New Testament Commentary Series. Grand Rapids, Mich.: Baker Book House, 1953, 1954.

Newbigin, Lesslie. *The Light Has Come: An Exposition of the Fourth Gospel.* Grand Rapids, Mich.: William B. Eerdmans Publishing Co., 1982.

IV. Topical Studies

Jacks, Bob and Betty, with Ron Wormser Sr. *Your Home, a Lighthouse.* Colorado Springs, Colo.: NavPress, 1986.

Kidd, Sue Monk. *God's Joyful Surprise: Finding Yourself Loved.* San Francisco, Calif.: Harper and Row, Publishers, 1987.

Larson, Bruce. *Living Beyond Our Fears: Discovering Life When You're Scared to Death.* San Francisco, Calif.: Harper and Row, Publishers, 1990.

Swindoll, Charles R. *Improving Your Serve: The Art of Unselfish Living.* Dallas, Tex.: Word Publishing, 1981.

Tournier, Paul. *The Strong and the Weak.* Trans. Edwin Hudson. Philadelphia, Pa.: Westminster Press, 1963.

Some of these books may be out of print and available only through a library. For those currently available, please contact your local Christian bookstore. Books by Charles R. Swindoll, as well as some books by other authors, may be obtained through Insight for Living.

Insight for Living also offers study guides on many books of the Bible, as well as on a variety of issues and biblical personalities. For more information, see the ordering instructions that follow and contact the office that serves you.

Notes

Notes

Notes

Notes

Notes

Ordering Information

Following Christ . . . The Man of God

If you would like to order additional study guides, purchase the cassette series that accompanies this guide, or request our product catalogs, please contact the office that serves you.

United States and International locations:

Insight for Living
Post Office Box 69000
Anaheim, CA 92817-0900
1-800-772-8888, 24 hours a day, seven days a week
(714) 575-5000, 8:00 A.M. to 4:30 P.M., Pacific time,
Monday to Friday

Canada:

Insight for Living Ministries
Post Office Box 2510
Vancouver, BC, Canada V6B 3W7
1-800-663-7639, 24 hours a day, seven days a week

Australia:

Insight for Living, Inc.
20 Albert Street
Blackburn, VIC 3130, Australia
Toll-free 1800-772-888 or (03) 9877-4277, 8:30 A.M. to 5:00 P.M.,
Monday to Friday

World Wide Web:

www.insight.org

Study Guide Subscription Program

Study guide subscriptions are available. Please call or write the office nearest you to find out how you can receive our study guides on a regular basis.